BOOST YOUR CAREER

WITH CHATGPT

The Ultimate Guide to AI in Job Searching

By

EBONY WASHINGTON

For permissions requests, please contact Work Life Win, Inc. at (347) 705-7768 or info@worklifewin.com.

Publisher's Cataloging-in-Publication data

Names: Washington, Ebony, author.
Title: Boost your career with ChatGPT : the ultimate guide to AI in job searching / Ebony Washington.
Description: New York, NY: Work Life Win, Inc., 2023.Identifiers: LCCN: 2023914427 | ISBN: 979-8-9888111-0-7 (paperback) | 979-8-9888111-1-4 (ebook) | 979-8-9888111-2-1 (audio)
Subjects: LCSH Job hunting--United States--Handbooks, manuals, etc. | Artificial intelligence. | Vocational guidance. | Occupations. | Résumés (Employment)--Handbooks, manuals, etc. | BISAC BUSINESS & ECONOMICS / Careers / General Classification: LCC HF5382.75.U6 .W37 2023 | DDC 650.14--dc23

First Edition

Published by

Work Life Win, Inc.
105 West 125th St Front 1 #1090
New York, NY 10027
United States
Phone: (347)705-7768
Email: info@worklifewin.com
Website: www.worklifewin.com

THIS BOOK IS DEDICATED TO

Mom, whose unwavering support has been a guiding light through all of my endeavors.

Shonte, for giving me my first opportunity in Human Resources and igniting my passion for career development.

Rick, who believed in me and hired me for my first job as a career advisor, shaping the trajectory of my professional journey.

Your belief in me has been a source of inspiration, and this book is a testament to the impact you've had on my career growth and development. Thank you for being an integral part of my career story.

"Technology can become the 'wings' that will allow the educational world to fly farther and faster than ever before — if we will allow it."

- *JENNY ARLEDGE*

CONTENTS

INTRODUCTION

Welcome to Boost Your Career with ChatGPT: The Ultimate Guide to AI in Job Searching. My name is Ebony, and I am your career coach with over twenty years of experience in workforce development. I began my career in human resources, reviewing countless resumes and meeting many job seekers who fell just short of getting the entry-level positions they desired. This inspired me to switch gears and work in career advisement, where I have worked in nonprofits, colleges, and now the city government, creating programs to help job seekers reach their full potential. Wanting to bring my expertise to a broader stage, I founded Work Life Win, Inc. to help those outside of my vicinity.

I work in New York City. Although the big apple is known for countless opportunities, it is also one of the most competitive job markets in the world, and I have helped my clients secure the jobs they desire and train for future roles. However, in recent years, the job search industry has undergone a significant shift with the introduction of artificial intelligence. This innovative technology has begun to function as a formidable gatekeeper, making it more challenging than ever to not only remain competitive but also ensure relevancy in this dynamic professional environment.

In the digital era, job search processes can be daunting, with intricate online application systems. In response to this, I have designed this book to guide you through these hurdles.

In the following pages, you will be introduced to ChatGPT, learning what it is and how it functions. You'll be walked through the process of setting up and using ChatGPT as a tool that can help you create resumes and cover letters that will make you stand out from the crowd.

The book also offers practical advice on how to use ChatGPT for interview preparation, industry, and company research, providing you with insight that will give you an edge in your job search. Moreover, the book addresses how to leverage ChatGPT for career planning, networking, and professional communication.

You will also learn about the importance of continuous learning and skill development and how ChatGPT can assist you in this aspect of your career progression. Furthermore, the book discusses potential limitations and ethical considerations of ChatGPT, providing you with a balanced view of the technology.

Finally, the content will help you understand how to embrace the future of job searching with AI. This book is designed for anyone, whether you're a recent graduate, considering a career shift, or simply exploring new opportunities.

Ready to go? Let's get started on this journey together.

Your Personal Guide: Navigating this Book for Your Job Search Journey

Ready to leverage AI in your job search? This book is designed to be as user-friendly as possible, with a structure that caters to your unique needs and circumstances. It's organized into chapters and subchapters, each focusing on a different aspect of how you can use ChatGPT in your job hunt.

If you're new to the world of AI and job searching, you might find it helpful to read the book from start to finish. This will give you a comprehensive understanding of ChatGPT and its many applications in the job market.

However, if you're looking for specific information or are already familiar with some aspects of AI, feel free to jump to the sections that are most relevant to your current stage in the job search process. Whether you're crafting your resume, preparing for an interview, or researching potential employers, there's a section designed to support you.

As you navigate through the book, you'll come across sections labeled "Career Prompt Master." These are your signposts for hands-on exercises and specific prompts to engage with ChatGPT. They'll help you apply the theory to practice and get the most out of ChatGPT for your job search.

Just remember, this book is here to serve you like a trusty sidekick in your career journey. It's your go-to resource to help you master the wave of AI in your job hunt. It's here to help you harness the power of AI and thrive in the modern job market. So, go ahead, take a look, and get ready to supercharge your job search! Let's get this show on the road!

CHAPTER 1
What is ChatGPT and How it Works

Understanding Artificial Intelligence and Machine Learning

Before we go into what ChatGPT is and how it works, it's essential to understand the underlying concepts that power it; namely artificial intelligence (AI) and machine learning (ML).

Artificial Intelligence refers to the capability of a machine to imitate intelligent human behavior. In other words, a broad area of computer science makes machines seem to possess human intelligence, including understanding human speech, competing in strategic games, or driving cars.

Imagine having a super smart assistant that can learn and solve problems, just like humans, without getting tired or needing a break. That's what AI is! It's like a brain but made up of computer code. It can do things like recognize speech, make decisions, and even learn from its mistakes. It's used in many places, from recommending what movie you should watch next on Netflix to helping doctors diagnose diseases.

Machine Learning, a subset of AI, is a method of data analysis that automates analytical model building. It's a system that can learn from data, identify patterns, and make decisions with minimal human intervention. Instead of explicitly programming an algorithm for a specific task, the machine is "trained" using large amounts of data and algorithms to give it the ability to learn how to perform the job.

Now, imagine if you could teach that super-smart assistant to get smarter over time. That's where machine learning comes in. It's a type of AI that can learn and improve from experience. Here's how it works: you give the machine lots of examples (like pictures of cats), and over time, it learns to recognize patterns (like what makes a cat a cat) and make predictions (like if a new picture is a cat or not).

In simpler terms, AI is like a smart assistant, and machine learning is the way we teach that assistant to get smarter over time. The beauty of this is that the more it learns, the better it gets at helping us solve problems and make decisions.

A Brief History and Development of ChatGPT

GPT stands for Generative Pretrained Transformer, a series of language processing AI models developed by OpenAI. ChatGPT, a variant of GPT, is explicitly designed to generate human-like text based on the text it's given.

The first version, GPT-1, was relatively simple but marked a significant AI and language processing breakthrough. Then came GPT-2, which was considerably more powerful and capable of generating surprisingly coherent and creative sentences. GPT-3, the third iteration, was even more advanced, demonstrating an impressive ability to produce human-like text. At the time of this book being written, the latest version is GPT-4, but future versions may exist beyond this date.

Its developers trained ChatGPT on a diverse range of internet text. It generates responses to text inputs by predicting what comes next in a conversation or text passage. However, it does not know specific documents or sources in its training set and cannot access or retrieve personal data unless explicitly provided during a conversation.

How ChatGPT Processes and Responds to Inputs

ChatGPT, an AI language model developed by OpenAI, is initially trained on an extensive collection of internet text. Despite its broad training base, it's important to remember that it doesn't know or have access to specific documents or sources.

When ChatGPT receives input—whether a question or a statement—it doesn't understand it as humans do. Instead, it dissects the sequence of words and discerns patterns within the input. Leveraging its training, it forecasts the next sequence of words by generating numerous potential options and assigning a probability to each. It then selects the most probable word, incorporates it into the context, and repeats this process to create a coherent response.

To refine its responses, OpenAI applies a secondary training process called fine-tuning. Human reviewers rate model outputs for an array of example inputs under specific guidelines, and the model generalizes from their feedback to generate responses to a wider variety of user inputs.

However, it's essential to understand that while ChatGPT can produce impressive, contextually relevant responses, it lacks human understanding of text, beliefs, or desires, and it doesn't access personal data about individuals unless shared in conversation. Its primary function is to predict and generate contextually relevant and coherent text.

Understanding the Capabilities of ChatGPT

ChatGPT is an incredibly versatile tool with numerous applications. Users can employ it to draft emails or other writing pieces, answer questions, tutor various subjects, translate languages, simulate characters for video games, and even generate Python code.

For your job search, you can leverage ChaGPT to create and refine resumes, simulate job interviews, research industries and companies, plan career paths, and draft professional communications in the context of job seeking.

However, while ChatGPT is powerful, it's not perfect. It doesn't understand text in the way humans do because it doesn't truly understand the world or have beliefs and desires.

It can't grasp context beyond the patterns it has learned, and unlike humans, it doesn't have personal experiences or beliefs to draw from. Also, although it can generate text that may seem emotionally resonant, ChatGPT does not experience or understand emotions.

Its responses largely depend on the input quality, meaning vague or incorrect input can lead to suboptimal output. It also lacks the ability to recall past interactions, treating each conversation as independent from the last.

Finally, while trained on a diverse dataset, ChatGPT doesn't have the capacity to fact-check or verify the information it generates. Therefore, despite its impressive capabilities, it's crucial to approach its outputs with an understanding of these limitations.

It simply predicts what should come next in a text based on patterns it learned during training.

In the following chapters, we will explore how you, as a job seeker, can harness the power of ChatGPT to enhance your job search and career development efforts.

CHAPTER 2
Setting Up and Using ChatGPT

How to Access ChatGPT

Accessing ChatGPT is relatively straightforward. You can interact with it through platforms and applications that have integrated it or by using the OpenAI API.

To use the OpenAI API, you must sign up for access, even with a usage fee. The following steps will guide you through this process. Please note that this process may change over time as OpenAI evolves its platform, here's the general process you would follow:

Step 1: Visit the OpenAI website

Navigate to the OpenAI website (https://www.openai.com) using your internet browser. OpenAI is the organization that developed ChatGPT, and all access to the model runs through their platform.

Step 2: Find the ChatGPT service

Once on the OpenAI website, find the section related to ChatGPT. As of 2021, you can generally access this from the "Products" or "Services" menu, but the website design may have changed. Look for references to GPT-3 or GPT-4, which are versions of the model used to power ChatGPT.

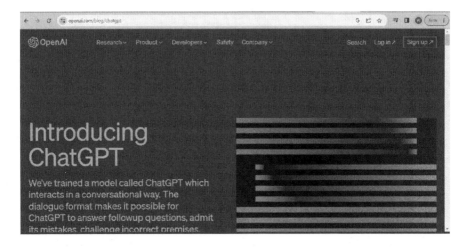

Step 3: Register an account

To use ChatGPT, you'll need to register for an account. Look for a button or link that says "Sign up" or "Register". You'll typically be asked to provide some basic information, such as your name, email address, and a password. Make sure to pick a secure password that you don't use on any other websites.

Create your account

Note that phone verification may be required for signup. Your number will only be used to verify your identity for security purposes.

info@worklifewin.com   Edit

Password

•••••••••••••

Your password must contain:

✓ At least 8 characters

Step 4: Confirm your email address

Once you've registered, OpenAI will likely send you an email to confirm your email address. Open this email and follow the instructions to confirm your address. This step helps OpenAI ensure that users are real people and protects the integrity of their system.

Step 5: API Key Generation

After registration and email confirmation, you may need to generate an API (Application Programming Interface) key. This key will be used to authenticate your requests to the ChatGPT service. You should keep this API key private and secure, just like a password.

Step 6: Usage Agreement

Ensure that you thoroughly read and understand the usage agreement and policies set by OpenAI for ChatGPT. It's important to use the service responsibly and within the guidelines and constraints that OpenAI has set.

Step 7: Set Up Billing

OpenAI usually provides a free tier for ChatGPT use but for intensive applications, you may need to opt for a paid plan. To set this up, you'll have to provide your payment information and choose your preferred billing cycle.

Once you've completed all of these steps, you'll have access to the powerful ChatGPT tool and can begin integrating it into your job search strategy.

Once you have access, you can send a series of messages to the ChatGPT endpoint, which will then return a model-generated message.

However, note that the exact steps and details may have changed or been updated refer to the official OpenAI website for the most current information.

Understanding Basic Features

ChatGPT is an effective tool for a range of text-generation tasks. Here are some of its key features.

Text Completion: Given a prompt, ChatGPT can generate a continuation, which can be a single sentence, a paragraph, or even a complete article.

Text Generation: You can provide a series of messages, and ChatGPT will generate a model message as a reply.

Language Translation: While not its primary function, you can use ChatGPT for translating text between languages.

Question Answering: You can ask ChatGPT questions to generate an answer based on its training data.

Summarization: ChatGPT can summarize long pieces of text. Like, say, an overly long job description.

Privacy and Security

Privacy and security are fundamental aspects of using AI technologies like ChatGPT. To this end, ChatGPT doesn't remember or store personal conversations, providing a layer of data privacy. It's designed to generate responses in real-time and can't recall or retrieve personal data from conversations.

OpenAI, the organization behind ChatGPT, implements measures to guard against potential cyber threats. Furthermore, ChatGPT is trained to avoid requests for personal data, which adds an extra layer of safety for users. Despite these safety measures, users should exercise discretion and caution when sharing information online.

It's important to remember that while ChatGPT is a powerful tool, it's crucial to use it responsibly. This includes being mindful of the information you're sharing with ChatGPT, or any digital platform. Prioritizing privacy and security is key to safely leveraging AI in your job search and broader digital interactions.

Ethics and Considerations of AI Usage

Data Privacy: As you interact with ChatGPT, remember that it can't remember or retrieve personal data from conversations unless explicitly provided in the conversation.

Misinformation: Since ChatGPT generates responses based on patterns in the data it was trained on, it might sometimes produce incorrect or misleading information. I know you've heard the story about the attorney who tried to construct his entire argument based on AI; well, all the cited cases were false. Be sure to fact-check.

Avoiding Inappropriate or Harmful Content: While safety mitigations have been implemented to prevent ChatGPT from producing harmful or inappropriate outputs, it may sometimes respond to harmful instructions or exhibit biased behavior.

Maintaining Coherent Long Conversations: ChatGPT's responses might lose coherence for longer conversations. It can start to repeat itself, contradict previous statements, or veer off-topic.

Dependence on AI: While ChatGPT can be an excellent tool, relying on it only partially is crucial. Remember to use your own judgment and skills.

As you begin using ChatGPT, consider these points to ensure you use the tool responsibly and effectively.

CHAPTER 3

Resume Creation with ChatGPT - Guidance on How to Structure a Resume

In the quest to secure your dream job, a well-crafted resume is a critical tool. Yet you may find the task of resume creation daunting, often needing help to present your experiences and skills compellingly and professionally. This chapter comes to your aid, introducing a transformative approach to resume design—leveraging the prowess of Artificial Intelligence. Specifically, we explore how OpenAI's powerful language model, ChatGPT, can assist you in building an impressive resume.

AI can significantly streamline the resume creation process, from detailing your contact information to highlighting your skills and experience. I will guide you through the nuances of each resume section, providing invaluable tips on using ChatGPT to enhance your resume's structure and content. We'll dive into practical examples, demonstrating how to collaborate with ChatGPT to draft compelling narratives for your career summaries, translate your raw job data into professional descriptions, and even optimize your list of skills and certifications.

Whether you are a seasoned professional looking to revamp your resume or a fresh graduate taking your first steps in the professional world, this guide offers a practical approach to unlocking your resume's full potential with AI's power. Let's embark on this exciting journey together!

Understanding ATS and Leveraging ChatGPT to Navigate Them

Applicant Tracking Systems (ATS) are software tools many employers use to automate the initial stages of the recruitment process. These systems scan resumes for relevant keywords, phrases, and other criteria outlined in the job description to identify the most promising candidates. An ATS acts as a filter, helping to hire managers to sift through large volumes of applications more efficiently.

However, ATS systems can also inadvertently overlook qualified candidates if their resumes are not precisely aligned with the specified criteria, even if they might fit the job well. This is where you can leverage the power of ChatGPT to your advantage.

1. Understanding ATS Keywords: The ATS ranks applicants based on the number and relevance of keywords matching the job description. ChatGPT can be of significant assistance in identifying these keywords. By providing the AI with the job description, you can ask it to highlight the critical skills, qualifications, and experience required.

With this information, you can ensure that you appropriately incorporate these keywords into your resume.

2. Formatting for ATS: Some ATS struggle with complex formats. Therefore, it's crucial to keep your resume layout simple and clean. ChatGPT can guide you in structuring your resume appropriately, suggesting ATS-friendly formats and reminding you to avoid headers, footers, and graphical elements that some ATS may not process correctly.

3. Tailoring Your Resume: As every job description is unique, customizing your resume for each application increases your chances of passing the ATS. ChatGPT can help tailor your resume by suggesting modifications to match each job's requirements. You can feed it the job description and your resume, then ask it to help adjust your resume to align better with the specific role.

4. Proofreading: ATS can be strict about spelling and grammar, as errors can cause a resume to be filtered out. ChatGPT can proofread your resume, helping ensure it's error-free.

ChatGPT can significantly assist in optimizing your resume for Applicant Tracking Systems (ATS), helping you identify and use relevant keywords, maintain ATS-friendly formatting, and tailor your content for specific job descriptions. However, it's important to note that no tool, including ChatGPT, can guarantee that a resume will pass through all ATS systems.

While ChatGPT can be a valuable ally in navigating ATS, remember that the ultimate decision-makers are humans. Always ensure that your resume is not just ATS-friendly but also appealing and easy to read for the hiring managers who will review it after it passes through the ATS.

AI-lluminating Resume Sections

Now that we understand how ATS works let's learn how a well-structured resume looks. Along the way, I'll add some prompts to assist you in developing your ATS-optimized resume. A standard resume usually contains the following sections:

Contact Information: ChatGPT can help ensure your contact information is formatted correctly and appears professional. For instance, you can ask whether the email address you're planning to use looks professional. You should also include your LinkedIn profile on your resume.

Objective or Summary: This is where ChatGPT really shines. You can brainstorm with the AI to generate a brief but compelling summary. To do this, provide details about your career goals, why you're applying for the role, and your unique qualifications. ChatGPT will help you structure this information into a concise, effective summary.

Experience: ChatGPT can help you generate professional descriptions of your past job responsibilities and achievements. Feed it your raw job data and ask it to draft professional summaries of your roles. You can ask it questions like "How can I phrase my experience as a project manager to highlight leadership and organizational skills?" or "How can I make my role as a sales representative sound more impactful?"

Education: While this section is typically straightforward, ChatGPT can help you determine how to format your educational history best, particularly if you have non-traditional educational experience such as online courses, boot camps, or internships.

Skills: If you need help deciding which skills to include on your resume, ChatGPT can assist. Provide it with a job description, and it can suggest what skills to highlight based on that description. You can ask, "What skills are typically required for a data analyst role?"

Certifications and Licenses: Similar to the Skills section, if you have several certifications and aren't sure which ones to include, ChatGPT can help you determine the most relevant ones based on the job description or the industry norms.

Awards and Honors: If you need help articulating your achievements professionally, ChatGPT can assist you. Describe the award and its significance, and it will help you present it in a professional light.

References: While it's becoming less common to include references on your resume, ChatGPT can provide guidance on how to format this section if you choose to include it. ChatGPT can also assist considerably with your resume's Publications and Social Media sections.

Publications: Here, the key is to present your work effectively and succinctly. ChatGPT can help generate a brief but comprehensive description for each publication. Start by providing details such as the publication's title, where it was published, its primary focus or argument, and its impact or reception. ChatGPT can then help you condense this information into a professional and concise format suitable for a resume. You can ask it questions like "How can I succinctly summarize this research paper for my resume?" or "What's a professional way to list my published book on my resume?"

Social Media: Adding your social media profiles, such as YouTube, to your resume can showcase a broader view of your professional persona. Let's say you are an accountant who gives tax advice; you can give your resume that professional boost, showcasing your knowledge and presentation skills. However, it's essential to describe your activity on these platforms professionally and relevantly. ChatGPT can assist you in crafting these descriptions. For a YouTube channel, ask questions like "How can I professionally summarize my YouTube channel's content, focusing on my tech tutorial videos?"

Remember, while ChatGPT can provide valuable suggestions, it's essential to ensure that the content of your social media profiles is professional, as potential employers may view them.

AI-mpress Employers Resume Optimization Steps

Now that we have an overview of some of the sections typical in a resume, here are my tips for using ChatGPT to enhance your resume. From the initial drafting stage to refining and customizing it for specific job descriptions; we'll explore how this powerful AI can assist you every step of the way.

Step 1 – Write your resume first: Before involving ChatGPT, you must draft your resume yourself to ensure that your experience, achievements, and skills are genuinely reflective of your abilities. Remember, while AI tools like ChatGPT can be incredibly creative, they can sometimes err toward fabrication. Hence, having a first draft written by you is vital to maintaining authenticity and accuracy.

Step 2 – Let ChatGPT Edit: After writing the initial draft, turn to ChatGPT for editing and refining. Beyond helping with individual sections, ChatGPT can also provide overall feedback on your resume. Once you've drafted your resume, ask the AI to review it for coherence, flow, and professionalism. It can suggest improvements and even proofread for grammar or spelling mistakes.

Step 3 – Write your resume for the job description: Tailoring your resume to each job description is a critical yet often overlooked step. While it may seem tedious, ChatGPT can significantly streamline this process. Feed your resume and the specific job description to the AI and ask it to help revise your resume accordingly. This allows you to effectively cater to the particular needs and language of each role you apply for.

Step 4 – Edit Again: After letting ChatGPT assist, carefully review the AI's output. Even though ChatGPT can provide highly relevant and professionally phrased content, human oversight is crucial to guarantee the accuracy and applicability of AI-generated content.

Resume Optimization Steps in Action

Now Let's put those tips for resume optimization in action. Take this general resume for Tiffany Jones, a mid-level social service worker.

Tiffany Jones

123 Main St, Anytown, USA | (123) 456-7890 | tiffany.jones@example.com LinkedIn: www.linkedin.com/in/tiffany-example-jones

Professional Summary

Dedicated and resourceful case manager with over five years of experience, including one year in a supervisory role. Proven track record in nonprofit and healthcare environments with expertise in managing caseloads, developing comprehensive plans for client recovery, and advocating for client needs. Strong commitment to treating clients with dignity and respect, contributing to a supportive and collaborative environment. Demonstrated ability to partner with interdisciplinary teams, providing exceptional coordination and administration skills.

Professional Experience

Senior Case Manager, Helping Hands Nonprofit, Anytown, USA | January 2022 - December 2022

- Oversaw a team of 5 case managers, providing supervision, guidance, and mentorship to ensure consistent and high-quality service delivery
- Managed a caseload of over 60 clients, delivering comprehensive case management services, including treatment planning, advocacy, and crisis intervention
- Fostered and maintained partnerships with community resources to facilitate client support and recovery
- Assisted with the development and implementation of a new case management process, leading to a 20% improvement in efficiency

Case Manager, Community Care Nonprofit, Anytown, USA | January 2020 - December 2021

- Worked closely with clients to identify their needs, goals, and potential barriers to success
- Coordinated with healthcare providers, social workers, and other resources to ensure continuity of care

- Developed, implemented, and evaluated service plans to ensure they met clients' needs and regulatory requirements
- Led bi-weekly professional development workshops for case management team to improve team skills and service delivery

Coordinator, Healthway Hospital, Anytown, USA | January 2019 – December 2019

- Facilitated coordination of care for hospital patients, working closely with physicians, nurses, social workers, and other healthcare professionals
- Acted as a liaison between patients, families, and healthcare teams, providing timely updates and ensuring seamless communication
- Assisted patients and their families with navigating complex healthcare systems, including insurance queries, outpatient services, and follow-up appointments
- Implemented a patient tracking system that improved patient follow-up care by 30%

Education

Master of Social Work, Anytown University, Anytown, USA | 2018 - 2020

Bachelor of Social Work, Anytown University, Anytown, USA | 2015 - 2018

Skills

- Team supervision and mentorship
- Patient advocacy
- Treatment planning
- Crisis intervention
- Excellent written and verbal communication
- Proficiency in Microsoft Office Suite and case management software

Certifications

Certified Case Manager (CCM), Commission for Case Manager Certification, 2020

Tiffany is an experienced case manager with a background in both non-profit organizations and healthcare, is seeking a supervisory role. She turns to Indeed.com and finds this job listing:

Clinical Supervisor

XYZ Nonprofit – NY, Queens

The Clinical Supervisor is responsible for the supervision of a clinical services housing team comprised of a licensed social worker and four case managers. Each staff manages a caseload of approximately 12 individuals who were formerly living on the street and in subways in New York City. This position has significant decision making, supervisory, administrative, program management, and service delivery responsibilities including but not limited to site management, program development, inter-team coordination, and contract/policy compliance. This person will be expected to participate in and contribute to a program culture that is client-centered, outcome-oriented, and dedicated to continuous quality improvement. The position requires a thorough understanding of relevant service delivery concepts and structures, including strong knowledge and experience working with the homeless population.

Responsibilities:

- Clinical and administrative supervision of day-to-day operations of the building and clinical services team
- Oversight of the program's contractual obligations
- Maintenance of appropriate staff levels to ensure consistent service delivery to clients
- Review of referrals from outreach teams and coordination of intake
- Collaboration with building management and security staff around maintenance and other site-related matters
- On-call support to the program during evening and weekend hours

Clinical Supervisor 1

- LMSW or Mental Health Counselor Limited Permit or Marriage and Family Therapy Limited Permit
- Relevant pre or post master's experience preferred
- Supervisory experience preferred

Clinical Supervisor 2

- LMSW or Mental Health Counselor Limited Permit or Marriage and Family Therapy Limited Permit
- 2 years relevant pre or post master's experience required
- Supervisory experience preferred

Clinical Supervisor 3

- LCSW, LMHC, LMFC
- Relevant pre or post master's experience in supervisory experienced preferred

OR

- LMSW or Mental Health Counselor Limited Permit or Marriage and Family Therapy Limited Permit
- 2 years supervisory experience in any field
- 4 years relevant experience in social services
- Supervisory experience in the field of housing or homeless services
- Strong crisis intervention skills
- Strong written and verbal communication skills and computer literacy
- Ability to interface effectively and efficiently with colleagues to ensure quality services and program operations.
- Commitment to utilization of a housing first and person-centered approach in working with clients
- Experience with DHS CARES preferred
- Bilingual English/Spanish preferred

***

How about we ask ChatGPT to revise it for the real-time job description.

Tiffany Jones

123 Main St, Anytown, USA | (123) 456-7890 | tiffany.jones@example.com

LinkedIn: www.linkedin.com/in/tiffany-example-jones

Professional Summary

Seasoned case manager turned clinical supervisor with a master's in social work and over six years of experience in non-profit and healthcare environments. Strong background in managing caseloads, developing comprehensive plans for client recovery, and advocating for client needs. Experienced in providing supervision and administrative coordination in housing and homeless services. Committed to a client-centered, outcome-oriented program culture with continuous quality improvement. Fluent in English and Spanish.

Professional Experience

Senior Case Manager, Helping Hands Nonprofit, Anytown, USA | January 2022 - December 2022

- Oversaw a team of 5 case managers, providing supervision, guidance, and mentorship to ensure consistent and high-quality service delivery
- Managed a caseload of over 60 formerly homeless individuals, delivering comprehensive case management services, including treatment planning, advocacy, and crisis intervention.
- Worked collaboratively with building management and security staff around maintenance and other site-related matters
- Coordinated intake and reviewed referrals from outreach teams
- Provided on-call support during evening and weekend hours

Case Manager, Community Care Nonprofit, Anytown, USA | January 2020 - December 2021

- Collaborated closely with clients to identify their needs, goals, and potential barriers to success
- Managed relationships with healthcare providers, social workers, and other resources to ensure continuity of care

- Led program development initiatives and ensured compliance with contractual obligations and policies
- Conducted bi-weekly professional development workshops for case management team to improve team skills and service delivery

Coordinator, Healthway Hospital, Anytown, USA | January 2019 - December 2019

- Coordinated care for hospital patients, acting as a liaison between patients, families, and healthcare teams
- Assisted patients and their families with navigating complex healthcare systems, including insurance queries, outpatient services, and follow-up appointments
- Implemented a patient tracking system that improved patient follow-up care by 30%

Education

Master of Social Work, Anytown University, Anytown, USA | 2018 - 2020

Bachelor of Social Work, Anytown University, Anytown, USA | 2015 - 2018

Skills

- Clinical and administrative supervision
- Team leadership and mentorship
- Crisis intervention
- Program development and contract compliance
- Strong written and verbal communication
- Proficiency in Microsoft Office Suite, case management software, and DHS CARES
- Bilingual (English/Spanish)

Certifications

Certified Case Manager (CCM), Commission for Case Manager Certification, 2020

Did you notice the five significant tweaks that illustrate the power of ChatGPT in optimizing a resume for a specific job? Let's break it down:

1. **Shaping the Professional Summary:** Did you see how the revised resume captures Tiffany's career shift from being a case manager to a clinical supervisor? Notice how her experience in housing and homeless services is highlighted. Is it evident how it underscores her dedication to the company culture the employer is seeking? And did you spot the bilingual skill - a definite plus-point listed in the job description?

2. **Adjusting Job Responsibilities:** When you peek into the 'Professional Experience' section, can you tell how the responsibilities from Tiffany's previous jobs are tweaked to echo the ones listed in the job description? For example, isn't it interesting that her coordination role for intake and outreach team referrals is explicitly stated? See how it syncs perfectly with the responsibilities of a Clinical Supervisor role?

3. **Injecting Relevant Details:** Did the revised resume catch your eye with details tailored to the job description? For example, notice how it pinpoints that Tiffany managed a caseload of over 60 formerly homeless individuals. Isn't that relevant considering the employer's anticipation of managing a similar caseload?

4. **Revamping Skills:** Are you keen on how the 'Skills' section is transformed to include verbatim from the job description? Like how "program development and contract compliance" found a place, and her bilingual ability gained emphasis?

5. **Spotlighting Certifications:** While the certification itself hasn't changed, did you notice how it's now more in line with the Clinical Supervisor role that Tiffany is applying for?

So, can you see how ChatGPT has fine-tuned Tiffany's resume, spotlighting her skills, experiences, and qualifications that perfectly align with the job description? See how this personalized approach could give you an edge in getting picked by potential employers?

Now let's look at Mark Sullivan, a marketing coordinator looking to level up into a managerial position.

Mark Sullivan

123 Anywhere St, Chicago, IL 60007
marksullivan@gmail.com
(123) 456-7890
 www.linkedin.com/in/mark-example-sullivan

Objective

Motivated and versatile Marketing Coordinator with 4 years of experience seeking to leverage proven skills in campaign management, market research, and content creation to drive marketing success. Known for enhancing overall brand presence and driving marketing initiatives that boost company visibility and profitability.

Skills

- Project management and team leadership
- Proficient in digital marketing and social media platforms
- Excellent communication and presentation skills
- Advanced skills in SEO and Google Analytics
- Proficient in MS Office, Adobe Creative Suite
- Strong analytical and problem-solving skills

Work Experience

Marketing Coordinator
ABC Company, Chicago, IL
July 2019 - Present

- Coordinated and managed 50+ marketing projects from concept to completion, driving increases in customer engagement by an average of 30%
- Conducted comprehensive market research and competitor analysis that influenced marketing strategy and boosted overall sales by 20%
- Supervised the creation and delivery of digital and print marketing materials, increasing brand recognition and customer reach

- Utilized Google Analytics to monitor and analyze website traffic, using findings to guide and optimize future marketing campaigns
- Led a team of 3 junior marketers, providing mentorship and direction to ensure the successful execution of marketing initiatives

Education

Bachelor of Science in Marketing
University of Illinois, Urbana-Champaign
Graduated May 2019

Certifications

- Google Analytics Certification – Google
- Certified Digital Marketing Professional – Digital Marketing Institute

References

Available upon request

While searching LinkedIn, he finds this exciting digital marketing manager position. Let's see how ChatGPT can revise the resume for this position.

Senior Digital Marketing Manager

Best Advertising Company Boston, MA Hybrid
Full-time
Senior Digital Marketing Manager at Best Advertising Company

Best Advertising Company is a full-service ad agency located in Boston, MA. We are gaining momentum and growing. Our environment is fun and collaborative. Everyone has input, and when something great happens, it is celebrated by all.

The senior digital marketing manager takes a lead role in planning, implementing, and optimizing digital marketing campaigns as a key member of Best's growing digital media team. As part of this role, the SDMM will work alongside the Media Director in leading strategy and execution. The right candidate will be inquisitive, motivated, and thrive in a culture of ongoing learning and problem solving.

Digital Marketing Campaign Leadership

- Scope and strategize digital marketing campaigns on various platforms including Programmatic and GDN Display, Native, Paid Social, YouTube, Paid Search, etc.
- Contribute to broader planning, strategy, and proposal documents.
- Attend select new business pitches.
- Work with account executives (AEs) to understand client goals and desired outcomes based on benchmarks and past campaign performance. Collaborate with AEs on storylines based on data and performance metrics.
- Interpret metrics for trends, successes, and opportunities.
- Own overall quality of end reporting result in terms of accuracy and actionable insights.
- Collaborate on cadence for reporting and updates for each unique campaign. This includes email updates, Google Data Studio dashboards, and PowerPoint presentations.
- Deliver timely results based on client needs, external influences, etc.
- Attend virtual and in-person client meetings to present metrics.
- Possess excellent time-management and communication skills.

- Have experience/familiarity with SEO and organic search strategy.
- Analyze user flow leveraging heatmapping tools such as HotJar and LuckyOrange.
- Leverage tools such as Google Analytics, Google Search Console, and SEMRush.

Paid Search Campaign Management

- Manage and optimize Google and Bing pay-per-click (PPC) campaigns.
- Identify budgets and original ad groups/campaigns for EVR clients.
- Perform campaign setup leveraging Google Campaign Manager and Google Tag Manager.
- Conduct paid search keyword research, text ad development, campaign management, and ongoing optimization.
- Execute and test different ad formats to obtain optimal conversion goals.
- Monitor paid search key performance indicators including search impression share and quality score in addition to core platform metrics, such as click-through rate, cost per click, and conversion rate.
- Provide historical analytics review for trend comparisons and determine search volume and relative competition/difficulty score as well as search trends.
- Suggest landing page optimizations for conversion-friendly PPC campaigns.
- Implement ideas and collaborate with broader team for A/B test schedules.

Required Skills and Experience:

- Bachelor's degree In Digital Marketing, Advertising, Communications, or related field.
- A minimum of five years of developing, managing, and implementing paid digital marketing and social campaigns.
- Strong knowledge of advertising and marketing trends and digital media strategy.
- Ability to multi-task, work under tight deadlines, and frequently adjust to changing priorities and timelines.

- Excellent written and verbal communication skills.
- Outstanding commitment to customer service.
- Proficiency with numbers, budgeting, and Excel.
- Ability to present ideas, problem solve, and negotiate.
- Exceptional attention to detail, organization, and time management.

Here's a revision of Mark Sullivan's resume tailored for the senior digital marketing manager position at Best Advertising Company:

Mark Sullivan

123 Anywhere St, Chicago, IL 60007
marksullivan@gmail.com
(123) 456-7890
www.linkedin.com/in/mark-example-sullivan

Objective

Highly experienced marketing professional with a passion for digital media and a track record of planning, implementing, and optimizing marketing campaigns. Seeking to leverage these skills and my leadership experience as a senior digital marketing manager at Best Advertising Company.

Skills

- Expertise in strategizing and managing digital marketing campaigns on various platforms
- Proficient in Google Analytics, Google Search Console, SEMRush, Google Campaign Manager, and Google Tag Manager
- Proficient in using heatmapping tools such as HotJar and LuckyOrange
- Strong familiarity with SEO and organic search strategy
- Outstanding communication, organization, and time management skills
- Proven ability to work under tight deadlines and adjust to changing priorities
- Strong knowledge of advertising, marketing trends, and digital media strategy

Work Experience

Marketing Coordinator

ABC Company, Chicago, IL
July 2019 - Present

- Led the planning, implementation, and optimization of over 50 digital marketing campaigns across platforms such as

Programmatic and GDN Display, Native, Paid Social, YouTube, and Paid Search
- Managed and optimized Google and Bing PPC campaigns, conducting keyword research, text ad development, and campaign management
- Worked with account executives to understand client goals and collaborate on data-driven storylines based on performance metrics
- Interpreted metrics for trends, successes, and opportunities, delivering timely results and actionable insights through reports and presentations
- Leveraged tools such as Google Analytics, Google Search Console, and SEMRush to analyze user flows and campaign performance

Education

Bachelor of Science in Marketing
University of Illinois, Urbana-Champaign
Graduated May 2019

Certifications

Google Analytics Certification – Google
Certified Digital Marketing Professional – Digital Marketing Institute

Let's explore the transformation of Mark Sullivan's resume together. Are you able to identify the five significant changes that have been made?

1. **Objective Refined:** First, notice how Mark's objective has been tailored to express his specific interest in the role of Senior Digital Marketing Manager at Best Advertising Company. Do you see how his experience with digital media and marketing campaigns shines through?

2. **Skills Amplified:** Look at how his skills have been reshaped to align with the job posting. Can you see the new additions -

familiarity with SEO and organic search strategy, strong knowledge of advertising and marketing trends, and how he has displayed his proficiency in using specific analytical tools?

3. **Work Experience Recontextualized:** How about the 'Work Experience' section? It now reflects his experience managing and optimizing PPC campaigns, along with his capacity to work with account executives and deliver results based on performance metrics. Can you sense how the language echoes the job description?

4. **Technology Tools Highlighted:** Mark's ability to use tools like Google Analytics, Google Search Console, and SEMRush is now clearly stated in his resume. Do you notice how these additions directly mirror the job requirements?

5. **Company Name Inserted:** Lastly, did you see how the revised resume specifies his desire to work at the "Best Advertising Company"? This sort of customization makes a resume more personal and shows that Mark has a keen interest in this particular company.

Did you catch these nuances? How these adjustments bring his resume closer to what the company is looking for in a Senior Digital Marketing Manager?

Now let's look at Maribelle Rodriguez, an ambitious recent graduate looking to leverage her Bachelor of Business Administration and leadership experience.

Maribelle Rodriguez

123 Main St, Austin, TX 78701
maribellerodriguez@gmail.com
(123) 456-7890

Objective

Detail-oriented and analytical recent BBA graduate seeking an entry-level Financial Analyst position. Brings strong understanding of financial principles from coursework and internships, coupled with leadership experience from student government and sorority involvement.

Education

Bachelor of Business Administration (BBA), Finance Concentration
University of Texas at Austin
Graduated May 2023

- Relevant Coursework: Corporate Finance, Investment Analysis, Financial Accounting, Financial Modeling, Statistics, and Economics.

Experience

Finance Intern

XYZ Corporation, Austin, TX
May 2022 - August 2022

- Assisted with financial forecasting and budgeting processes, resulting in more accurate financial planning
- Prepared financial reports and participated in quarterly and annual closing processes
- Collaborated with the finance team to analyze financial data and identify cost-saving opportunities

Finance Intern
ABC Company, Austin, TX
May 2021 - August 2021

- Supported the preparation of financial analyses and reports for senior management
- Conducted research and data analysis to aid in strategic decision-making
- Assisted in the development of financial models to evaluate potential investment opportunities

Leadership Experience

President
XYZ Sorority, University of Texas at Austin
May 2022 - May 2023

- Led a team of 10 executive board members and oversaw the sorority's operations, impacting over 100 members
- Managed budget planning, event management, and member recruitment, resulting in a 20% increase in membership

Treasurer
Student Government Association, University of Texas at Austin
May 2022 - May 2023

- Managed a budget of $200,000 and ensured accurate tracking of all financial transactions
- Presented financial updates at monthly meetings and made recommendations for budget allocations

Skills

- Proficient in Microsoft Excel, PowerPoint, and Word
- Knowledge of financial modeling and forecasting
- Strong analytical and problem-solving skills
- Excellent written and verbal communication skills
- Detail-oriented with excellent organizational skills

References

Available upon request

This resume highlights Maribelle's relevant coursework, internships, and leadership roles, showing both her academic and practical preparation for an entry-level Financial Analyst position.

Maribelle sets up her LinkedIn account to search for entry-level positions and found this Junior Financial Analyst position.

Junior Financial Analyst

Health Provider, LLC Troy, MI On-site
$55,000/yr. - $80,000/yr. · Full-time
Junior Financial Analyst at Health Provider, LLC

About the job

If you enjoy analyzing data and are looking for that opportunity to dive into a growing business and help drive financial projections and models based on data analysis and business partnership interaction, then this may be the perfect role for you. Health Provider is currently seeking a Junior Financial Analyst (JFA) to work alongside our Senior Financial Analyst and the rest of the Finance Department. This role involves focusing on budget planning, actual to forecasted results analysis, and performance optimization. This individual will utilize their finance skillset and develop their ability to dig deep and summarize key points and results. This role requires some interaction with leadership, supports services leaders, and requires strong communication and presentation skills.

Under the supervision of the Senior Financial Analyst, the JFA is responsible for analyzing, reporting, and aggregating organizational datasets, providing the finance and operating departments with information and analytic support for the business lines. The successful candidate will partner with all divisions and departments of the organization to analyze, mine, understand, and interpret the financial and operational data. This position plays a critical role in providing management an assessment of historical and forward-looking financial performance, including analysis of variances and trends, risks and opportunities, and communication of insights. The role requires strong organization and communication skills while maintaining attention to detail in a fast-paced environment.

The ability to efficiently and effectively update, analyze, monitor, and run multiple scenarios on large data sets is critical. While this is **classified as an entry-level position**, applicants with some level of experience are welcome to apply; the pay scale for this position is based on experience and technical proficiency.

Responsibilities:

- Support the Revenue Recognition and Revenue Analysis Needs Monthly
- Meet with departmental leaders to build annual budget
- Review monthly actual results to forecast in detail and discuss any significant or unusual variances
- Provide results presentation monthly for consolidation into the monthly earnings package
- Assist with long term planning
- Build financial models for strategic initiatives
- Support and attend senior leadership and board results presentations
- Support requests for ad-hoc financial analysis

Requirements:

- Bachelor's degree in accounting, finance, or related business major
- 0-3 years' experience in a financial analyst or related role
- Expert level in use of Excel
- Moderate to highly skilled in SQL, Alteryx, Microsoft Power BI
- Excellent communication (written and verbal) skills, customer service, and organizational skills
- Strong communication skills
- Excellent work habits

Here's a revised version of Maribelle's resume specifically for the Junior Financial Analyst position at Health Provider, LLC:

Maribelle Rodriguez

123 Main St, Austin, TX 78701
maribellerodriguez@gmail.com
(123) 456-7890

Objective

Detail-oriented and analytical BBA graduate seeking a Junior Financial Analyst position. Brings strong understanding of financial principles from coursework and internships, along with leadership experience and proficiency in Excel, SQL, and Power BI.

Education

Bachelor of Business Administration (BBA), Finance Concentration

University of Texas at Austin
Graduated May 2023

- Relevant Coursework: Corporate Finance, Investment Analysis, Financial Accounting, Financial Modeling, Statistics, and Economics

Experience

Finance Intern

XYZ Corporation, Austin, TX
May 2022 - August 2022

- Assisted in analyzing financial data for budget planning and forecasting, providing actionable insights for strategic decisions
- Prepared and presented monthly earnings packages to senior management
- Utilized Excel and SQL to manage and analyze large datasets, enhancing the accuracy of financial forecasting

Finance Intern

ABC Company, Austin, TX
May 2021 - August 2021

44

- Supported the creation of financial models to evaluate strategic initiatives
- Assisted in reviewing monthly actual results to forecast, identify, and discuss significant variances
- Utilized Power BI to visualize financial data and trends, improving understanding and decision-making for senior management

Leadership Experience

President
XYZ Sorority, University of Texas at Austin
May 2022 - May 2023

- Managed budget planning and financial transactions for the sorority, improving financial efficiency and transparency
- Collaborated with diverse teams to organize events and recruit members, demonstrating strong communication and organizational skills

Treasurer
Student Government Association, University of Texas at Austin
May 2022 - May 2023

- Managed a budget of $200,000, conducted financial analysis and reported on variances and trends
- Presented financial updates at monthly meetings, utilizing effective communication and presentation skills

Skills

- Expert proficiency in Microsoft Excel
- Moderate to high proficiency in SQL and Microsoft Power BI
- Strong analytical and problem-solving skills
- Excellent written and verbal communication skills
- Detail-oriented with excellent organizational skills

References

Available upon request

Let's take a look at how Maribelle's resume has evolved to better fit the Junior Financial Analyst role:

1. **Starting Point:** In her updated resume, Maribelle gets straight to the point in her objective statement - she's going after a Junior Financial Analyst position. Plus, she gives a nod to her skills in Excel, SQL, and Power BI right off the bat.

2. **Internship Adventures:** Maribelle's internship experiences in the revised resume are not just impressive, they're tailor-made for this job! From budget planning to financial forecasting, and from preparing earnings packages to using Excel and SQL for data analysis, her internship duties line up perfectly with the job requirements.

3. **Leader, Not a Follower:** Maribelle's updated resume tells the story of a leader. It frames her past roles and responsibilities to highlight experiences that are super relevant to her dream job, like managing budgets, dealing with financial transactions, and presenting financial updates.

Career Prompt Master: Ready for some Algorithmic Assistance? Try out these prompts:

1. "How can I make my resume summary more compelling?"
2. "What's a professional way to describe my experience as a [job title]?"
3. "What skills are typically required for a [desired job title] role?"
4. "How can I highlight my achievements in my role as a [job title]?"
5. "Can you suggest a better way to present my education credentials?"
6. "Which certifications would be most relevant for a [desired job title] role?"
7. "How can I describe my publications in a professional manner?"
8. "Can you help me list my awards and honors in an impressive way?"
9. "What's a professional way to summarize my LinkedIn activities for my resume?"
10. "How can I professionally describe the content of my YouTube channel?"

Now get those job descriptions ready! Here are some prompts you can use with ChatGPT to create an ATS-friendly resume:

1. "Identify the key skills and qualifications in this job description."
2. "Suggest how I can incorporate these keywords into my resume."
3. "What is an ATS-friendly format for my resume?"
4. "How can I tailor my resume for this specific job description?"
5. "Can you suggest changes to my resume that align better with this job's requirements?"
6. "Proofread my resume for any spelling or grammar errors."

7. "What sections or elements should I avoid in my resume to make it more ATS-friendly?"

8. "Review my resume and suggest improvements to make it more compatible with ATS systems."

9. "Can you suggest action verbs I can use in my resume that ATS systems might favor?"

10. "What buzzwords or industry jargon from this job description should I include in my resume?"

Constantly review and consider its suggestions carefully, ensuring they align with your personal style and the standards of your industry. Additionally, it's always a good idea to have a human, particularly one familiar with your industry, review your resume before sending it out.

And with that, you're well on your way to creating an effective resume with the help of ChatGPT!

CHAPTER 4

Soaring Through Cover Letters with AI: Harnessing Your Potential Word by Word

In Chapter 3, we delved into the complexities of Applicant Tracking Systems (ATS) and outlined a step-by-step approach for navigating these digital gatekeepers. With the assistance of AI, particularly our trusty ChatGPT, we learned how to take a primary resume draft and transform it into a polished document uniquely tailored for your dream job.

As we forge ahead into cover letters, we'll adopt a similar strategy, breaking down the process into digestible sections. This helps you understand how to create the most compelling cover letter possible. And, of course, keep an eye out for our "Career Prompt Master," who will provide excellent prompts for developing your resume and cover letter.

The body of your cover letter is your chance to present compelling examples and achievements that directly showcase your suitability for the role. Here are some guidelines on the types of examples you might include:

Relevant Skills: Discuss instances where you used key skills required for the job. If the job requires strong customer service skills, describe a time you went above and beyond to help a customer.

Achievements: Quantified achievements are especially compelling. You might discuss hitting or exceeding your targets if you're in sales. If you're in project management, highlight completing a project ahead of schedule or under budget.

Initiative and Leadership: Demonstrate times when you took the initiative to solve a problem or led a team to success.

Relevant Work Experience: Provide examples from your work history demonstrating your ability to perform the job you're applying to successfully. Discuss specific tasks and projects you've worked on similar to those you'd be taking on in the new job.

Learning Experiences: If you're a new graduate or changing careers, discuss experiences where you learned or demonstrated transferable skills. This might be a class project, internship, or volunteer experience.

Here are a few ways you could prompt ChatGPT to help you generate these examples:

- "ChatGPT, how can I showcase my leadership skills in my cover letter based on my experience leading a team project at my previous job?"
- "ChatGPT, I exceeded my sales targets for four consecutive quarters. How can I incorporate this achievement into my cover letter for a sales manager position?"

- "ChatGPT, I implemented a new software system in my last job that increased productivity. How can I describe this experience in a cover letter for a project manager role?"

Remember, the goal is to choose examples that directly align with the job requirements, as these will be most compelling to the hiring manager.

Cover letters allow you to introduce yourself, demonstrate your interest in a position, and explain why you're the ideal candidate. Much like with your resume, ChatGPT can assist in crafting compelling cover letters.

AI-Assisted Greeting: Your First Digital Handshake

Your cover letter begins with a professional greeting. While this might seem straightforward, it sets the tone for your letter. ChatGPT can provide suggestions on how to address the hiring manager professionally if their name is known or suggest general professional greetings when it isn't.

AI Introduction: Launching Your Letter's Mission

The introduction is your first chance to grab the reader's attention. Here, ChatGPT can assist in drafting an engaging introduction that explains why you're applying. Provide the AI with a brief overview of the job you're applying for, your essential qualifications, and why you're interested in the role. It can then help generate a catchy yet professional introduction for your cover letter.

AI Body: Powering Through Your Qualifications

The body of your cover letter is where you provide specific examples of how your qualifications align with the role. Feeding ChatGPT information about your previous roles, achievements, and skills can generate text that effectively conveys how you meet the job's requirements. The AI can also help structure this section to ensure it flows well and remains engaging to the reader.

AI Closing: Landing Your Letter Smoothly

The closing of your cover letter is equally important, as it leaves the final impression. ChatGPT can assist in crafting a solid conclusion that effectively summarizes your interest in the role and encourages the reader to review your attached resume.

AI Review: Ensuring Your Cover Letter is Ready for Liftoff

While ChatGPT is a powerful tool for drafting and refining your cover letter, it's important to review the AI-generated content to ensure it accurately represents your qualifications and aligns with the specific job you're applying for. This step is vital to ensure that your personal voice is present in the letter and that the content accurately represents you as a professional.

Just like with your resume, tailoring your cover letter to each job description is a key step. ChatGPT can streamline this process, assisting you in making the necessary modifications to suit each role you apply for.

AI-Crafted Cover Letters - Illuminating our 3 Job Seeker's Cover Letters

If you recall from Chapter 3, we utilized ChatGPT to craft an impressive resume for Tiffany Jones, a dedicated social services worker seeking to make a greater impact. Given her refined resume, tailored specifically for the prospective role at XYZ Healthcare, Tiffany is now ready to complement it with a compelling cover letter.

Let's revisit Tiffany's journey. We have already asked ChatGPT to revamp her resume and align her past experiences with the job requirements at XYZ Healthcare. In this chapter, we're taking it a step further by employing the AI's capabilities to create a persuasive cover letter. This will not only highlight her competencies and passion but also articulate why she is a strong fit for this specific role. So, let's see how ChatGPT can support us in this endeavor.

[Your Name]

[Your Address]

[City, State, ZIP]

[Your Email]

[Today's Date]

Dear Hiring Manager,

I am writing to express my interest in the social services supervisor position at XYZ Healthcare, as advertised. With my strong background in social work and case management, coupled with my passion for advocating for the welfare of individuals, I am confident in my ability to make significant contributions to your team.

One of the most rewarding aspects of my work has been advocating for clients and ensuring their needs are met with dignity and respect. My passion for the work that I do extends to the collaborative environment I strive to create with my colleagues. I believe in the value of interdisciplinary collaboration to provide comprehensive support for clients and have seen firsthand how this approach can lead to more effective and efficient care.

XYZ Healthcare's commitment to providing quality care for its residents deeply resonates with me. I am familiar with your organization's work and reputation in the community, and I admire how you bring together diverse professionals to create a holistic care environment for your residents. I am excited about the opportunity to bring my expertise, values, and dedication to a respected organization like XYZ Healthcare.

I look forward to the opportunity to further discuss how my background, skills, and passion for social work align with the needs and values of your organization.

Thank you for considering my application.

Sincerely,

Tiffany Jones

As demonstrated, ChatGPT skillfully curated a compelling cover letter, further accentuating Tiffany Jones' professional narrative. This is a testament to the power of AI in streamlining the job application process and highlighting the unique experiences of job seekers.

Now let's revisit Mark Sullivan, our creative marketing coordinator looking to level up into a managerial position. First, let's examine his general cover letter.

Here's a revised version of the cover letter for Mark, tailored to a marketing manager position:

Mark Sullivan

123 Anywhere St, Chicago, IL 60007
marksullivan@gmail.com
(123) 456-7890

June 12, 2023

Dear Hiring Manager,

I am writing to express my interest in the marketing manager position within your esteemed organization. With 4 years of experience as a marketing coordinator, honing skills in project management, team leadership, and strategic marketing initiatives, I believe I am well equipped to take on the challenges of this role.

In my current role as a marketing coordinator at ABC Company, I have successfully managed over 50 diverse marketing projects, driving a significant increase in customer engagement by 30% on average. I spearheaded comprehensive market research and competitor analysis, directly influencing our marketing strategy and leading to a boost in sales by 20%. I believe these accomplishments illustrate my ability to drive the success of large-scale marketing initiatives.

In addition to the technical aspects of marketing, I am particularly proud of my leadership contributions. I have led a team of junior marketers, instilling in them a sense of purpose, direction, and motivation. These leadership experiences, I believe, have been instrumental in preparing me for the managerial responsibilities that come with the position for which I am applying.

I am also adept in various digital marketing tools, such as SEO and Google Analytics, having obtained relevant certifications. My proficiency in these tools, coupled with my capacity for data-driven decision-making, will be valuable in strategizing, executing, and assessing the effectiveness of marketing campaigns.

Joining your organization as a marketing manager presents an exciting opportunity for me to leverage my skills and experiences to contribute to your ongoing success. I am passionate about leading a team toward the execution of innovative and impactful marketing strategies. Thank you for considering my application. I look forward to the opportunity to discuss how my background, skills, and passion for marketing could benefit your organization.

Sincerely,

Mark Sullivan

This version of the cover letter is more targeted toward a marketing manager position, highlighting Mark's leadership experience and strategic accomplishments in his current role.

Now, here's a revised version of the cover letter for Mark, specifically customized to the senior digital marketing manager position at Best Advertising:

Mark Sullivan

123 Anywhere St, Chicago, IL 60007
marksullivan@gmail.com
(123) 456-7890

June 12, 2023

Dear Hiring Manager,

I am writing to express my interest in the senior digital marketing manager position at Best Advertising Company. With 4 years of hands-on experience in planning, implementing, and optimizing digital marketing campaigns, I am prepared to bring a strong understanding of digital media strategy and a proven leadership approach to your team.

In my current role as a marketing coordinator at ABC Company, I have managed and optimized numerous digital marketing campaigns across various platforms, including Programmatic, GDN Display, Native, Paid Social, YouTube, and Paid Search. My comprehensive experience in campaign management has led to a significant increase in customer engagement and overall sales for our clients.

I bring an exceptional proficiency in tools such as Google Analytics, Google Search Console, SEMRush, Google Campaign Manager, and Google Tag Manager. I have used these tools to deliver timely, data-driven insights and actionable recommendations to our clients. Additionally, I am familiar with SEO and organic search strategy, which would be beneficial in achieving Best Advertising's digital marketing objectives.

Moreover, I am confident in my ability to work collaboratively with account executives to understand client goals, strategize campaigns, and deliver results based on data and performance metrics. My strong communication skills have always enabled me to present metrics effectively in both virtual and in-person meetings.

Best Advertising's commitment to continuous learning and problem-solving aligns with my professional ethos. I am excited about the opportunity to bring my digital marketing expertise, commitment to customer service, and passion for problem-solving to the senior digital marketing manager role.

Thank you for considering my application. I look forward to the possibility of discussing how my experience and skills can contribute to the growth and success of Best Advertising Company.

Sincerely,

Mark Sullivan

This version of the cover letter is more targeted toward the senior digital marketing manager position at Best Advertising Company, highlighting Mark's relevant experiences, his understanding of the required tools, and his ability to work under the described work conditions.

What differences did you notice?

Finally, here's a general cover letter for Maribelle Rodriguez, our ambitious recent grad looking to break into finance:

Maribelle Rodriguez

123 Main St, Austin, TX 78701
maribellerodriguez@gmail.com
(123) 456-7890

[Today's Date]

Dear Hiring Manager,

I am writing to express my interest in your open Financial Analyst position. As a recent graduate with a Bachelor of Business Administration, a concentration in finance, and hands-on experience through two financial internships, I am well-equipped to make a significant contribution to your team.

During my internships at XYZ Corporation and ABC Company, I gained substantial experience in forecasting, budgeting, and data analysis. I collaborated with experienced finance teams to develop models and prepare reports, providing me with a deep understanding of the complexities of operations within a corporate setting.

In addition to my practical experience, I completed rigorous coursework in corporate finance, investment analysis, and financial modeling. This academic background, coupled with my proficiency in Microsoft Excel, has equipped me with the tools to effectively analyze data and contribute to strategic decision-making processes.

In addition to my academic and professional experiences, I have honed my leadership and teamwork skills through my involvement in XYZ Sorority and the Student Government Association at the University of Texas at Austin. As president of my sorority and treasurer of the student government, I gained valuable experience in budget management and collaborative decision-making.

I am excited about the opportunity to bring my analytical skills, attention to detail, and passion for finance to an entry-level financial analyst position. I am confident that my unique blend of experiences and skills makes me a strong candidate for this position.

Thank you for considering my application. I look forward to the opportunity to discuss how my educational background, internship experiences, and leadership roles have prepared me to contribute to your team.

Sincerely,

Maribelle Rodriguez

This cover letter emphasizes Maribelle's academic background, practical experience from her internships, and leadership roles, demonstrating her readiness for an entry-level financial analyst position.

Here's a tailored cover letter for Maribelle Rodriguez for the junior financial analyst position at Health Provider, LLC:

Maribelle Rodriguez

123 Main St, Austin, TX 78701
maribellerodriguez@gmail.com
(123) 456-7890

[Today's Date]

Dear Hiring Manager,

I am excited to apply for the junior financial analyst position at Health Provider, LLC, as advertised. As a recent Bachelor of Business Administration graduate with a concentration in finance, with hands-on experience through internships at XYZ Corporation and ABC Company, I believe my analytical skills, attention to detail, and proficiency in tools such as Excel, SQL, and Power BI make me an excellent candidate for this role.

During my internships, I had the opportunity to engage in financial data analysis for budget planning and forecasting. This allowed me to contribute to strategic decision-making processes and gain hands-on experience with financial modeling. Furthermore, I frequently utilized tools like Excel and SQL to manage and analyze large datasets, and Power BI for data visualization. These experiences have not only enhanced my technical proficiency but also honed my ability to communicate complex financial information clearly and effectively.

In addition to my internships, my academic background in finance has equipped me with a strong understanding of financial principles. My coursework included areas such as corporate finance, investment analysis, and financial modeling, all of which are directly relevant to the responsibilities of the junior financial analyst role.

Beyond my academic and professional qualifications, I have developed leadership and communication skills through roles as president of my sorority and treasurer of the student government at the University of Texas at Austin. These roles demanded meticulous financial management, strong organizational skills, and effective communication—abilities I am eager to apply in a professional context.

I am excited about the opportunity to support Health Provider, LLC in driving financial projections, building models, and optimizing performance. I am confident that my blend of technical skills, academic knowledge, and leadership experience has prepared me well for this role.

Thank you for considering my application. I look forward to the possibility of contributing to your team and am eager to discuss my qualifications in more detail.

Sincerely,

Maribelle Rodriguez

This cover letter emphasizes Maribelle's relevant academic and practical experience, proficiency in the necessary tools, and her communication and leadership skills, all tailored to the specific requirements of the junior financial analyst position she is applying for.

Career Prompt Master: Let's Make the Most out of That Cover Letter

Cover letters allow us to elaborate on our unique stories, highlighting not just our experiences and skills but our passion and commitment to the roles we seek. In this next exercise, I have prepared ten prompts designed to tap into ChatGPT's capabilities to help us craft persuasive, professional, personalized cover letters.

So, without further ado, let's take on the exercise and elevate our cover letter crafting skills to new heights!

- "ChatGPT, I'm applying for a data analyst position at a tech company. How can I start my cover letter to engage the hiring manager right away?"
- "ChatGPT, I have five years of experience in digital marketing, with a focus on SEO. Can you help me draft a compelling paragraph for my cover letter showcasing this experience?"
- "I want to express my passion for the nonprofit sector in my cover letter. Can you help me articulate this effectively?"
- "ChatGPT, I'm transitioning from a career in journalism to public relations. Can you help me write a section in my cover letter that connects my past experience to my future role?"
- "I'm looking to highlight my project management skills in my cover letter for a software engineering role. Can you assist me in crafting a paragraph for this?"
- "ChatGPT, I have a certification in graphic design that I want to mention in my cover letter for a design role. How can I do this professionally?"

- "I have successfully led a team of five in my previous role. Can you help me describe this leadership experience in my cover letter?"
- "ChatGPT, how can I conclude my cover letter to leave a strong impression and prompt the hiring manager to review my resume?"
- "I need to write a cover letter for a remote position. How can I express that I am self-motivated and disciplined in my work habits?"
- "ChatGPT, I want to add a personal touch to my cover letter without sounding unprofessional. Can you suggest a way to do this?"

Fresh Perspectives & Career Pivots: ChatGPT's Aid for New Grads and Career-Changers

Now let's address the unique challenges for those navigating the job market as a new graduate or as someone seeking a career change. Fortunately, ChatGPT can be a valuable companion on this journey, helping you tailor your application materials to represent your potential or transferable skills best. Let's explore some specific ways ChatGPT can assist you:

New Graduates:

As a new graduate, you may feel that your lack of experience is a stumbling block. However, you likely have more relevant skills and experiences than you realize, and ChatGPT can help you highlight these. ChatGPT can help articulate how your academic achievements, internships, research projects, or even extracurricular activities can contribute to the role you're applying for.

Here are some prompts you can use:

- "ChatGPT, I've recently graduated with a degree in computer science, and I'm looking to apply for a software developer position. In my cover letter, how can I highlight my academic projects and internship experiences?"
- "ChatGPT, as a new graduate with a degree in business administration, how can I make my leadership roles in university clubs relevant in my cover letter for a project management role?"

Career Changers:

If you're seeking a career change, your challenge is to connect your past experiences to your desired role, even if they seem unrelated. ChatGPT can help you identify and articulate transferable skills and experiences that can make you a strong candidate.

Here are some prompts you can use:

- "ChatGPT, I'm transitioning from a teaching career to a career in corporate training. How can I demonstrate the transferability of my skills in my cover letter?"
- "ChatGPT, I'm moving from a career in finance to one in tech sales. How can I write a cover letter that highlights my transferable skills and experiences?"

Sidestepping Common Pitfalls: Maximizing Your Cover Letter's Impact with ChatGPT

Cover letters are a critical piece of your job application process. They provide an opportunity to make a personalized connection with hiring managers and demonstrate why you're a perfect fit for the role. However, several common mistakes can undermine the effectiveness of your cover letter. Here, we'll explore some of these pitfalls and see how ChatGPT can help avoid them.

Mistake 1: Using Generic Language

Using generic or boilerplate language can make your cover letter feel impersonal and unconvincing.

ChatGPT can assist you in customizing your cover letter to make it more targeted and engaging. Provide ChatGPT with specific details about the job and the company and ask it to generate a draft tailored to these details.

- Prompt example: "ChatGPT, I'm applying for a project management role at XYZ Tech, a company known for its innovative approach to software development. Can you help me draft a unique and targeted cover letter?"

Mistake 2: Neglecting Proper Formatting and Grammar

Improperly formatted cover letters or those with grammatical errors can leave a negative impression.

ChatGPT can help ensure that your cover letter is not only well-structured but also free from grammatical mistakes. Ask ChatGPT to review your cover letter for errors and provide suggestions for improvements.

- Prompt example: "ChatGPT, can you help me review this cover letter and suggest any grammatical or formatting corrections?"

Mistake 3: Overusing Buzzwords or Industry Jargon

While it's important to speak the language of your industry, overusing buzzwords or jargon can make your cover letter feel insincere or hard to understand.

ChatGPT can assist in ensuring that your cover letter is clear, concise, and accessible while still using industry-specific language appropriately. Provide your cover letter to ChatGPT and ask for feedback on clarity and use of jargon.

- Prompt example: "ChatGPT, can you review my cover letter and suggest where I might be overusing industry jargon or buzzwords?"

By utilizing ChatGPT, you can avoid these common pitfalls and craft a more compelling, engaging cover letter.

Remember, the journey to finding a job, whether as a new graduate or a career changer, can be filled with uncertainty. However, with the right tools like ChatGPT, you can successfully communicate your value and potential to prospective employers.

However, remember always to have the final say. After all, no one knows your qualifications and aspirations better than you do!

CHAPTER 5
Interview Preparation with ChatGPT

Utilizing ChatGPT for Common Interview Questions

Preparing for an interview involves anticipating the questions that will be asked and rehearsing articulate, thoughtful responses. ChatGPT can be invaluable in this process because it can generate human-like text.

ChatGPT can list common interview questions for your specific industry or role. This could range from general questions like "Tell me about yourself" and "Why do you want this job?" to more role-specific inquiries. Once you have this list, you can rehearse your responses and even ask ChatGPT to critique or enhance your answers.

Common Interview Questions

Regardless of the industry, some questions are almost universally asked during interviews. ChatGPT can help you prepare for these by formulating and refining your responses. Let's Start with those common interview questions.

Certain questions are frequently asked across various industries during interviews. Below are a few examples:

- Tell me about yourself.
- Why are you interested in this role?
- Where do you see yourself in five years?
- What are your strengths and weaknesses?
- Why should we hire you?

You should expect and have prepared responses for these questions, as they often form the backbone of many interviews. However, avoid memorizing responses verbatim, as they may appear rehearsed and impersonal. Instead, focus on the key points you want to convey in each answer.

ChatGPT can assist in crafting personalized and effective responses. Provide the AI with your background, experiences, and job role you're interviewing for, and request help formulating responses.

Prompt example: "ChatGPT, I'm a software developer with five years of experience in a startup. I'm interviewing for a senior developer role at a larger tech company. How can I effectively answer the " Tell me about yourself" question?"

Tackling Industry-Specific Questions with ChatGPT

Industry-specific questions are a significant part of any job interview. They are the hiring team's way of gauging your skill set, technical knowledge, and understanding of the role in question. These can range from questions about your hands-on experience in certain situations, your approach to problem-solving, or your familiarity with industry trends and tools.

Harnessing ChatGPT's Power for Industry-Specific Questions

ChatGPT can be a powerful resource to help you prepare for these more specialized questions. Here's how:

Identifying Relevant Questions: If you're unsure what industry-specific questions might arise, ask ChatGPT. For example, "What questions might be asked in an interview for a data science role?"

Crafting Responses: Once you have a set of potential questions, you can use ChatGPT to help craft your responses. For example, "ChatGPT, how should I respond to a question about my experience with machine learning algorithms in a data science interview?"

Explaining Technical Terms: If there are technical aspects of the job that you're not fully comfortable with, ChatGPT can provide explanations. For instance, "What is the role of neural networks in deep learning?"

Role-Playing Interviews: Use ChatGPT to simulate an interview. Provide the job description and your resume, then request a mock interview. You can then practice responding to the AI's questions.

Practical Application: Data Analyst Example

Take a practical example: you're applying for a data analyst role. One common question might be: "Can you describe a time when you used data to drive business strategy?"

To help formulate a response, provide ChatGPT with relevant details about a time you used data to inform business strategy. For instance, you might say, "ChatGPT, I once used sales data to identify underperforming products and recommended marketing strategies that increased their sales by 20%. How can I frame this experience effectively in an interview?"

While the prospect of industry-specific questions can be daunting, remember that they are an opportunity to showcase your expertise and passion for your field. Using ChatGPT to prepare, you can approach these questions confidently and clearly, leaving a strong impression on your interviewers.

Different industries and roles will have specific questions relating to the required skills and knowledge. Here are some examples of industry-specific questions that you might prepare for using ChatGPT:

Tech Industry (Software Developer Role)

- Can you describe your experience with programming languages?
- How do you handle debugging and error handling?
- Can you discuss a project you've worked on and the development methodologies you used?

Healthcare Industry (Nurse Role)

- How do you handle stressful situations and high-pressure environments?
- Can you provide an example of when you had to handle a difficult patient situation?
- What specific experience do you have with electronic health records?

Finance Industry (Financial Analyst Role)

- How would you assess the financial health of a company?
- Can you describe a time when you used data analysis to inform a financial decision?
- How do you stay updated on changes in financial regulations and standards?

You can ask ChatGPT to generate a list of common interview questions for your industry and then use it to practice and refine your responses. For role-specific inquiries, you can also use ChatGPT to get a sense of the technical questions you might be asked so that you can prepare accordingly.

AI-Assisted Employer Reconnaissance: Using ChatGPT to Navigate Company Research

When considering a job opportunity, it's imperative to conduct thorough research on the potential employer. This due diligence involves understanding the company's mission, values, culture, products or services, market position, and reputation. Comprehensive research equips you with the knowledge to answer interview questions confidently and helps you gauge if the company aligns with your professional and personal values.

While ChatGPT doesn't have access to specific documents or real-time information about companies due to its data cutoff in September 2021, it can still provide significant assistance during this crucial phase of your job hunt. Here's how:

Deciphering Mission Statements and Values: Company mission statements and core values can often be laden with jargon or abstract ideas. You can ask ChatGPT to explain the general principles behind common corporate values or mission statement language. For instance, "ChatGPT, what does it mean when a company says they value 'innovation'?"

Understanding Industry Landscape: ChatGPT can give you a general overview of different industries based on its extensive training data. For example, if you're applying for a job in the renewable energy sector, you can ask, "ChatGPT, what are the current trends in the renewable energy sector?"

Assessing Company Culture: You can ask ChatGPT about the significance of different aspects of company culture and what they might mean for you as a potential employee. For example, "ChatGPT, what does it mean if a company emphasizes a 'flat hierarchy' and 'open-door policy'?"

Identifying Red Flags: ChatGPT can advise on potential red flags to look for during your research or the interview process. For instance, "ChatGPT, what are some warning signs of a toxic work environment?"

Formulating Questions: When you have a job interview, it's a good practice to have a list of questions for the potential employer. You can ask ChatGPT to help you generate insightful questions based on your understanding of the company. For example, "ChatGPT, based on a company mission focused on sustainability and community involvement, what are some good questions I can ask during my interview?"

ChatGPT can be a valuable ally in your company research phase, helping you understand the nuances of corporate language, the implications of company culture, and generating thoughtful questions for your interviewers. By leveraging AI, you can go beyond surface-level understanding and gain deeper insights into your potential future workplace.

AI Guided Futurecasting: Leveraging ChatGPT for Understanding Industry Trends

Staying current with industry trends is crucial to navigating your career trajectory successfully. It helps you understand where your industry is heading, what skills are in demand, and what potential challenges might emerge in your field.

Though ChatGPT can't provide real-time updates on industry trends due to its data cutoff in September 2021, it can still be a valuable tool to enhance your comprehension of evolving industries. Here's how:

Generating Relevant Questions: ChatGPT can help generate probing questions that you should ask when researching current industry trends. For instance, you can ask, "ChatGPT, what are some critical questions to ask when researching trends in the renewable energy sector?"

Understanding Impact Factors: ChatGPT can guide you in assessing the implications of various factors on industry trends, such as new technologies, regulatory changes, economic indicators, and more. For example, "ChatGPT, how do regulatory changes generally impact the healthcare industry?"

Evaluating Technological Advancements: Technological changes drive many industries. ChatGPT can help you understand the potential impact of various technologies on your industry. For example, "ChatGPT, how has AI impacted the finance industry?"

Predicting Skills in Demand: ChatGPT can assist you in understanding which skills were in high demand based on past and current trends. For instance, "ChatGPT, what skills were becoming important in digital marketing as of 2021?"

While ChatGPT is an insightful guide for understanding industry trends and their implications, it's essential to supplement this guidance with real-time analysis using current resources, industry reports, news updates, and databases. Combining AI insights and timely information allows you to keep your finger on the pulse of your industry's changing landscape.

Career Prompt Master: Let's Get Ready for that Interview

Greetings from the Career Prompt Master once again! Interviews can be nerve-wracking, but preparation can make a world of difference. These ten prompts will guide you to generate insightful responses to common interview questions:

- "ChatGPT, how can I best describe my experience when asked, 'Tell me about yourself?'"
- "What's a compelling way to explain my interest in the role when asked, 'Why are you interested in this role?'"
- "ChatGPT, can you help me craft a future-focused, realistic answer for 'Where do you see yourself in five years?'"
- "I need to address the question 'What are your strengths and weaknesses?' Can you help me structure balanced and honest responses?"
- "ChatGPT, help me to convincingly articulate 'Why should we hire you?' in relation to my skills and the job requirements."
- "I'm applying for a project manager role. How should I respond to 'How do you handle a missed deadline?'"
- "ChatGPT, I'm interviewing for a customer service position. Could you assist me in crafting a response to 'How do you handle difficult customers?'"
- "I will be interviewing for a data analyst position. How should I answer 'Can you describe a time when you used data to solve a problem?'"
- "ChatGPT, help me develop an answer for 'Can you describe a time you had to make a difficult decision at work and what was the outcome?'"

- "I'm applying for a sales role. Could you guide me in answering 'How do you handle rejection?' in the context of unsuccessful sales attempts?"

You can feed ChatGPT with the job description and ask it to dream up some interview questions. It's like having your own personal interview coach! Give it a shot; it could really level up your interview prep!

Conquering the AI Arena: Mastering Interview Prep

So, there we have it—using ChatGPT as your interview coach, you can navigate common interview questions, answer industry-specific queries, and even learn to understand the ins and outs of potential employers and industry trends.

Remember, the key to success lies in preparation. Use the prompts from our trusty "Career Prompt Master," practice your responses, and conduct thorough research. The synergy of your knowledge and ChatGPT's capabilities can provide a significant edge in your job quest.

As with the other stages of job hunting, always bring your critical thinking skills into play. Review ChatGPT's responses, personalize them to suit your unique experiences and voice, and ensure they're always authentic.

By embracing AI in your interview prep, you're not just getting ready for one interview—you're gearing up to conquer the ever-evolving career landscape of the 21st century. So, go forth, future interview superstar—the world is waiting for your success.

CHAPTER 6
Using ChatGPT for Industry and Company Research

Mastering the AI Matrix: Demystifying the Job Market

In the previous chapter, we highlighted the importance of understanding your potential employers and industry trends during your interview prep. Now, it's time to dig deeper. Grasping the nuances of the job market is a crucial facet of any successful job hunt. It encompasses in-depth research about your desired industries, discerning the in-demand skills and qualifications, and an overall understanding of the employment terrain.

Although ChatGPT lacks real-time access to databases or the ability to trawl the internet for current information, it's designed to generate text based on patterns learned from an extensive range of internet text during its training phase. This means it can offer general advice on scrutinizing the job market, which factors you should consider, and how to tailor your job search strategy to align with these factors.

Understanding the job market is key, whether you're just starting your career, planning a transition, or looking for your next great opportunity. But remember, the job market isn't static—it's a constantly shifting landscape that demands ongoing research and adaptability. Don't worry; ChatGPT is your AI ally; you're well-equipped to navigate this matrix and find your perfect fit. Stay tuned for the "Career Prompt Master's" cues on how you can utilize ChatGPT effectively to gain insights into the job market dynamics.

AI and the Art of Company Sleuthing: A Guide to Researching Potential Employers with ChatGPT

Understanding potential employers becomes pivotal as you venture deeper into your job search. This extends beyond merely recognizing the company's name or being vaguely aware of what they do. It's about delving into their mission, values, work culture, products or services, and overall reputation.

ChatGPT does not have direct access to specific documents or sources due to its training data limitations. However, you can leverage it to craft insightful questions and identify key areas to explore during your employer research. When researching a potential employer, you can ask general questions about the factors you should consider. For instance, why is understanding a company's culture important? How can you interpret a company's mission and values about your own career goals? What signs could indicate a company's stability and growth trajectory?

Whether it's a small startup or a global conglomerate, every organization has a unique footprint. By asking the right questions and knowing what to look for, you can better align your career aspirations with a company's ethos and future direction. ChatGPT, with its broad spectrum of linguistic understanding, can help guide you through this process, ensuring your approach to company research is as comprehensive and effective as possible.

Stay tuned for the "Career Prompt Master's" handy tips on how to harness ChatGPT for your company sleuthing mission.

AI-Assisted Transition: Charting a Course into Data Science with ChatGPT

Let's look at a specific example of how you can apply these tools. Consider for a moment that you're looking into transitioning into the field of data science and specifically eyeing roles at a tech company like Meta. Here's how you could use ChatGPT.

Understanding the Job Market: You could start by asking ChatGPT, "What are the key skills generally required for a data scientist?" or "What are the emerging trends in data science?" While it's crucial to remember that ChatGPT cannot provide real-time data or updates, it can give an excellent overview of the usual requirements and trends based on its training data.

Researching the Employer: When researching Meta, you could prompt ChatGPT by asking, "What are some important factors to consider when researching a tech company like Meta?" or "What are some common aspects of culture in tech companies?" Again, it's important to note that ChatGPT won't know specific documents or sources about Meta from its training data, but it can provide a general framework for what to look for based on patterns it learned during its training.

Tailoring Your Application: You could ask ChatGPT, "What points should I emphasize in my cover letter for a data science role at a tech company?" or "How can I tailor my resume to better fit a data science position?"

Now, let's hear from the Career Prompt Master.

Career Prompt Master: Mastering the AI Art of Company Recon: Career Prompt Master's Wisdom for Company Research

Greetings again from the Career Prompt Master! Company research often seems daunting, but don't worry; I've got your back. Here are a few prompts to guide your reconnaissance mission with ChatGPT and help you better understand your prospective employers:

- "ChatGPT, what are some key aspects to consider when researching a company's culture?"
- "ChatGPT, can you explain why understanding a company's mission and values is important during job hunting?"
- "How can I assess a company's growth potential, ChatGPT?"
- "What are some potential red flags when researching a company's reputation, ChatGPT?"
- "ChatGPT, how does the size of a company potentially impact its work culture and my role?"
- "What questions should I ask during an interview to better understand a company's management style, ChatGPT?"
- "ChatGPT, can you guide me on interpreting a company's financial health from publicly available reports?"
- "How might a company's industry affect its stability and growth potential, ChatGPT?"
- "ChatGPT, what types of employee benefits and policies should I look for when researching a company?"
- "How can I understand a company's stance on diversity and inclusion, ChatGPT?"

Remember, these prompts are just the beginning. Use them as a launchpad to unearth your prospective employer's landscape. Understanding a company's ethos, growth, and culture means you're taking an informed step toward a fulfilling career. Happy hunting!

Cross-Referencing for Success: Integrating AI Insights with Real-Time Data Sources

It's beneficial to pair the capabilities of ChatGPT with external resources. While ChatGPT provides a broad understanding and can generate general advice based on patterns it has learned, it's crucial to cross-verify with reliable resources for the most accurate, up-to-date information.

O*NET OnLine: This is an excellent resource for learning about different occupations. It includes information about necessary skills, education, and even typical tasks and activities associated with each job. It also provides data on wages and employment trends.

Bureau of Labor Statistics (BLS): The BLS provides a broad range of statistics related to the U.S. labor market. Here, you can find information on unemployment rates, wage trends, and much more. A particularly useful resource is the Occupational Outlook Handbook, which provides comprehensive information about hundreds of occupations, including projected job growth.

U.S. Department of Labor (DOL): The DOL provides a wealth of resources on various topics including job training, wages, and worker's rights. They also have a section dedicated to career exploration and job analysis.

Company Websites: Most companies have websites that provide information about their current operations, corporate culture, and strategic focus. This is an excellent resource to better understand the company you're interested in. The 'careers' or 'jobs' section typically includes job postings and descriptions, giving insight into the skills and qualifications they're looking for.

LinkedIn: This is a professional networking site where users can create profiles and connect with other professionals. You can view company pages, see job postings, and gain insights from current and former employees about the company culture and operations. LinkedIn also provides salary insights for different roles and industries.

Glassdoor: Glassdoor is another valuable resource for job market research. It provides company reviews from employees, salary data, and job listings. It can give you a sense of what it's like to work at a particular company, as reported by the people who have actually worked there.

Indeed: Indeed is a comprehensive job search engine. You can find job postings, company reviews, and salary information. They also provide a variety of resources to aid in your job search, including resume creation and interview tips.

Economic Policy Institute (EPI): EPI conducts research and analysis on the economic status of working America. It provides reports and briefings on a range of topics, including wages, jobs, unemployment, and labor policy.

Pew Research Center: Pew Research conducts public opinion polling, demographic research, media content analysis, and other empirical social science research. It's a good source for understanding broader social trends that can impact the labor market.

Remember that labor market research can vary by country. The resources listed here are primarily for the United States, but similar organizations and tools exist in most countries. Always make sure the information is recent, relevant, and reliable.

Here's how you can leverage these sources along with ChatGPT.

ChatGPT's Guide to Navigating the Job Market: Closing Thoughts

As we wrap up this chapter on understanding the job market, it's important to recognize that while ChatGPT is a powerful tool, it's part of a bigger toolkit. It can provide you with insights and guidance and help generate creative thoughts around market trends, company culture, and potential interview questions. However, your active participation, intuition, and real-time research are equally crucial.

The magic happens when you harmoniously blend AI insights with your personal experiences, industry knowledge, and research findings from credible, real-time resources. You are the real driver in this journey, and ChatGPT is your co-pilot, ready to assist whenever you need it.

As we navigate the winding roads of job markets and employer research, remember to take the wheel, engage your curiosity, and be ready to explore new paths that ChatGPT's AI-powered insights might illuminate. But also, keep your eyes on the road and use real-time data and resources to validate these insights.

By synergizing AI's capabilities with your active effort, you can significantly enhance your understanding of the job market, making your job search more focused, efficient, and, hopefully, successful.

On to the next chapter, where we'll continue exploring ways of using ChatGPT in your career planning!

CHAPTER 7
Career Planning with ChatGPT

AI-Assisted Journey: Career Mapping Reimagined

Career mapping is a strategic approach to professional growth. It involves outlining your career aspirations, the milestones you aim to achieve, and the path to reach these goals. This could encompass identifying requisite skills, planning for roles to aim for, and establishing a realistic timeline for career progression.

ChatGPT can function as an intelligent companion in this endeavor. Here's how you can leverage AI to optimize your career mapping:

1. Clarifying Career Goals with AI: Begin by communicating your career objectives to ChatGPT. It could be as broad as wanting to be a leader in the tech industry or as specific as aiming to be a data science manager at a leading tech firm within five years. Once ChatGPT understands your goals, it can provide insights or questions to help clarify and solidify these goals.

2. Charting a Course with AI: After understanding your career goals, ask ChatGPT to suggest potential steps to reach these objectives.

This could include acquiring new skills, gaining specific experience, or even aiming for intermediate roles that could pave the way toward your ultimate goal.

3. Skills Identification with AI: Depending upon your targeted role or industry, there will be certain skills that you will need to acquire or develop. ChatGPT can help suggest these skills based on your career aspirations.

4. Milestone Planning with AI: Career progression is often not linear but comprises various milestones. ChatGPT can help you identify these milestones and suggest a realistic timeline to achieve them.

Unfolding New Horizons: ChatGPT as Your Guide in Exploring Career Paths

One of the crucial facets of career planning is the exploration of potential career paths. Your interests, skills, aspirations, and even curiosity might lead you to contemplate multiple career avenues.

ChatGPT can be a supportive partner in this exploratory journey. Let's look at how AI can contribute to expanding your career vista:

1. Deep Diving into Roles with AI: You can ask ChatGPT to furnish detailed information about various roles you're curious about. This could include understanding typical responsibilities, skills required, or even the potential challenges and rewards linked to these roles.

2. Surfacing Industry Insights with AI: Every industry has its own distinct career trajectories. You could prompt ChatGPT to generate a list of roles commonly pursued in a particular industry or to shed light on the industry's growth potential, emerging roles, and trends.

3. Navigating Career Transitions with AI: Career transitions within the same industry or across different ones could be complex and require careful planning. ChatGPT can provide insights into what such transitions could entail, including the possible challenges, skills required, and strategies for success.

4. Seeking Career Inspiration with AI: You could also utilize ChatGPT for brainstorming. For example, asking ChatGPT to suggest unconventional or emerging roles based on your skill set and interests might spark new career ideas you hadn't considered before.

In essence, ChatGPT can serve as a personalized, readily available resource for exploring career paths. As always, remember to complement the advice from ChatGPT with your own research and real-time data. AI can help illuminate potential paths, but the journey and destination are for you to decide!

How to Have Career Conversations with AI

Having career conversations with ChatGPT can help you refine your thoughts, articulate your goals, and consider different perspectives. For instance, you might share your current career situation and goals and ask ChatGPT for advice on how to achieve those goals. Or you might ask ChatGPT to generate questions that could help you reflect on your interests, strengths, and areas for growth.

Remember, however, that while ChatGPT can generate thoughtful and insightful text, it doesn't understand your situation or the context in the way a human career counselor would. So, while it can be a valuable tool for career planning, its advice should be considered along with other resources and personalized guidance.

AI-Powered Reflections: Career Conversations with ChatGPT

Navigating the labyrinth of career planning often calls for deep introspection, clear articulation of goals, and exploration of various possibilities. Having career conversations with an AI like ChatGPT can be an interesting way to facilitate these processes. Let's see how:

1. Illuminating Your Pathway with AI: Share your current career situation and aspirations with ChatGPT, then ask for its advice on how to achieve those goals. While ChatGPT doesn't understand your situation as a human would, it can provide insights based on patterns and models it has learned. This can help you see your career path from a fresh perspective.

2. Reflective Questioning with AI: Use ChatGPT to generate thought-provoking questions that encourage you to reflect on your interests, strengths, potential blind spots, and areas for growth. Such reflective exercises can aid in self-awareness, an essential component of effective career planning.

3. Considering Different Perspectives with AI: You could present ChatGPT with hypothetical situations or dilemmas you might encounter in your career journey and ask for advice. This can help you anticipate possible challenges and consider diverse solutions.

However, it's vital to remember that while ChatGPT can be a helpful tool in career planning, it should not be the sole counselor. It doesn't possess the human understanding or the real-time knowledge that a career counselor would have.

Case Study: From Novice to Guru - Career Mapping in the AI Industry with ChatGPT

Meet Jane Nguyen, a recent computer science graduate looking to break into the rapidly growing field of artificial intelligence (AI). While she has foundational knowledge and has worked on a few AI projects during her degree, she's unsure about the career path she should follow to achieve her dream of becoming a leading AI researcher. Let's see how she uses ChatGPT to navigate her career journey.

1. Clarifying Career Goals: Jane starts by sharing her long-term career goal with ChatGPT: to become a leading AI researcher. ChatGPT suggests potential steps to reach this goal, such as pursuing advanced degrees, gaining practical experience in AI projects, publishing research papers, and networking in the AI community.

2. Exploring Career Paths: To understand the breadth of AI roles, Jane asks ChatGPT to describe various positions in the AI industry, their typical responsibilities, and their qualifications. ChatGPT provides insights into roles like AI Engineer, Data Scientist, Machine Learning Engineer, and AI Research Scientist, along with the skills required for each. Jane finds this information invaluable in helping her visualize the progression from her current position toward her desired role.

93

3. Role-Playing Career Conversations: Jane simulates a career conversation with ChatGPT. She outlines her current situation: a fresh graduate with a computer science degree and a keen interest in AI. She shares her long-term goal and asks for advice on the steps she could take to get there. ChatGPT suggests potential short-term goals, like getting a job as an entry-level AI engineer, enrolling in a master's degree, or contributing to open-source AI projects to gain practical experience.

4. Anticipating Challenges: Jane uses ChatGPT to brainstorm possible challenges she might face on her career path, such as keeping up with the rapidly evolving AI field. ChatGPT suggests strategies like continuous learning, attending AI conferences, and subscribing to AI research journals.

Through this process, Jane not only gains clarity about her career path but also feels more prepared and confident. She understands that while ChatGPT can provide valuable insights and suggestions, the final decision rests with her, considering her unique situation, interests, and aspirations. Jane continues to use ChatGPT as a resource as she takes her first steps into the exciting world of AI.

AI Intervention: Unveiling the Career Prompt Master's Career Mapping Secrets

Welcome back, dear reader! It's your friendly Career Prompt Master here, ready to aid you once again in your quest to harness the power of AI in career planning. This time, we're tackling the vast world of career mapping. Navigating the countless possibilities may seem daunting, but fear not! With ChatGPT at your side and my carefully crafted prompts in your arsenal, we'll be charting a course to your dream job in no time.

As you know, ChatGPT is like a chatbot librarian, ready to provide guidance based on a wealth of past training data. But remember, it's not psychic! To get the most out of your AI companion, be clear, specific, and detailed in your prompts.

Ready? Here are ten prompts designed to help you create a detailed, actionable career map. Enjoy the journey, and may your career dreams become a reality!

Clarifying Goals: "ChatGPT, I want to become a leading AI researcher. What could be the potential steps or milestones to achieve this goal?"

Career Path Exploration: "ChatGPT, could you describe the roles in the AI industry and their typical responsibilities and qualifications?"

Career Conversations: "ChatGPT, I am a fresh computer science graduate interested in AI. What advice would you give to reach my goal of becoming an AI researcher?"

Skill Analysis: "ChatGPT, based on my current skills and interests, what AI roles could be a good fit for me?"

Navigating Challenges: "ChatGPT, what challenges might I face in my journey to becoming an AI researcher, and how could I overcome them?"

Networking Advice: "ChatGPT, how can I effectively network in the AI industry?"

Continuing Education: "ChatGPT, should I consider further education like a master's or Ph.D. to advance in the AI field?"

Day in the Life: "ChatGPT, could you describe a typical day in the life of an AI researcher?"

Career Progression: "ChatGPT, what does a typical career progression look like in the AI industry?"

Career Switch: "ChatGPT; I'm currently working as a software engineer. How can I transition to an AI role?"

Use these prompts to help navigate your career-mapping conversations with ChatGPT.

CHAPTER 8
Networking and Professional Communication with ChatGPT

Using ChatGPT to Draft Professional Emails

In today's digital age, email is a primary form of communication, especially in the professional world. However, drafting the perfect professional email can be time-consuming and sometimes daunting. That's where ChatGPT comes in. It can help you draft professional emails by saving time and ensuring your message is clear, concise, and appropriately formatted.

How to Use ChatGPT for Professional Emails

1. Provide Context

To begin, you need to provide ChatGPT with context for the email. This should include the purpose of the email and the key points you wish to have. For example, suppose you're writing a follow-up email after a job interview. In that case, you might tell ChatGPT, "I want to thank the interviewer for their time, express my continued interest in the position, and ask about the next steps in the hiring process."

2. Let ChatGPT Generate a Draft

After providing the necessary context, ChatGPT will generate a draft of the email for you. Remember, this is a machine learning model, so it will use the information you provide to generate the most appropriate response.

3. Review and Edit the Draft

Once ChatGPT has generated the draft email, review and edit it to ensure it aligns with your voice and the tone you wish to convey. Double-check all information, including names, job titles, and specific details about the job or company.

4. Send Your Email

After you've reviewed and edited your email, it's ready to be sent! You've just saved time and mental effort by having ChatGPT assist you in drafting a professional email.

Examples of Emails ChatGPT Can Help With

ChatGPT can be used to draft a variety of professional emails, including:

Job applications: Craft a compelling email to accompany your resume and cover letter when applying for a job.

Networking: Reach out to professionals in your industry to build relationships, ask for advice, or seek job opportunities.

Follow-up emails: Send a follow-up email after an interview to thank the interviewer and express continued interest.

Client communications: Communicate effectively with clients by drafting clear and concise emails.

Remember, using AI to draft your emails does not replace the personal touch that comes from crafting an email yourself. Use AI as a tool to assist in the process, saving you time and helping you maintain a professional tone. Always review and personalize AI-generated emails before sending them out.

AI-Mazing Correspondence: Powered by ChatGPT, Tailored by You

To give you a taste, I've guided ChatGPT to create a series of sample letters tailored to various professional contexts. So, please peruse at your convenience, and explore the potential of AI-enhanced professional correspondence.

Here are some examples of letters I prompted ChatGPT to write for different professional circumstances...

Subject: Request for Insight on Upcoming Interview at [Company Name] - [Your Name]

Dear [Recipient's Name],

I hope this message finds you well. My name is [Your Name], and I am a fellow alumnus of [Your Alma Mater]. I graduated in [Your Graduation Year] with a degree in [Your Major] and found your profile through our alumni network.

I'm reaching out because you currently work at [Company Name] in the [high-demand sector], a field I am highly interested in and passionate about. I'm excited to share that I have an interview scheduled next week for the [Job Title] position at [Company Name]. It would be invaluable to hear from someone like you who has firsthand experience at the company.

If you have the time, would you be open to a brief conversation to share some insights about the company culture, the [high-demand sector] industry, and any advice you might have for the interview process? Any information you could provide would be beneficial as I prepare for the interview.

I understand that you have a busy schedule, and I appreciate any time you can spare. Please let me know if there's a convenient time for you in the coming days. I am flexible and can accommodate a phone call, video call, or even a quick chat over coffee if you prefer.

Thank you in advance for considering my request. I look forward to connecting with you and learning from your experiences at [Company Name].

Best regards,

[Your Name] [Your LinkedIn profile link] [Your Contact Information]

Subject: Great Meeting You at [Networking Event Name] – [Your Name]

Dear [Colleague's Name],

I hope this message finds you well. I wanted to say how much I enjoyed meeting you at the [Networking Event Name] last [day, i.e., Tuesday]. Our conversation about [specific topic you discussed] was truly insightful and gave me valuable takeaways.

Your extensive experience in [colleague's industry or role] and thoughts on [specific point discussed] were particularly enlightening. I found your perspective on [reiterate a particular topic you discussed] to be deeply interesting, and it has prompted me to consider this issue in a new light.

If you're open to it, I would love to continue our conversation about [topic] over a coffee or lunch sometime soon. Also, if I can be of help to you, please do not hesitate to ask.

I've added you on LinkedIn, and I hope to keep in touch. It's always great to meet like-minded professionals in [your industry], and there is much more we can learn from each other.

Thank you again for your time and the meaningful conversation. I look forward to our paths crossing again soon.

Best regards,

[Your Name] [Your LinkedIn profile link] [Your Contact Information]

Subject: Reflecting on Our Discussion at [Networking Event Name] – [Your Name]

Dear [Colleague's Name],

I hope this message finds you well. I am reaching out to express how much I appreciated our conversation at the [Networking Event Name] this past [day, i.e., Tuesday]. Our engaging discussion about [specific topic you discussed] provided me with some valuable insights.

Your depth of knowledge in [colleague's industry or role], and the unique perspective you shared on [specific point discussed], were both enlightening and inspiring. I found your views on [reiterate a particular topic you discussed] especially thought-provoking, and it has stimulated some new thinking on my part.

I would welcome the opportunity to continue our conversation about [topic] in a more informal setting, perhaps over a coffee or lunch if you're amenable. Additionally, I'd like to extend an offer of assistance in any area where you might find my input or skills beneficial.

I have sent you a LinkedIn connection request, hoping that we can maintain this professional relationship. Connections like ours are what make [your industry] such an engaging field, and there's more we can learn from each other.

Thank you again for your invaluable insights and the stimulating discussion. I am eagerly looking forward to our next interaction.

Best regards,

[Your Name] [Your LinkedIn profile link] [Your Contact Information]

Notice any similarities? They all start with the phrase, "I hope this message finds you well." Get rid of it! Here is where personalization comes into play. You'll pick up on other similarities the more you use ChatGPT.

Boosting Online Professional Presence with AI: ChatGPT's Role

In today's digitized professional landscape, maintaining an impressive online presence has become crucial. It's a powerful tool to improve your visibility among potential employers, foster networking opportunities with professionals in your field, and showcase your skills and achievements. This presence often extends beyond a well-crafted LinkedIn profile to include a professional website, industry-specific online platforms, or even a personal blog discussing industry trends and insights.

While ChatGPT isn't designed to interact directly with these platforms or construct profiles for you, its capabilities as a language model make it a valuable tool for creating polished content for your online presence. From drafting articulate LinkedIn summaries to generating insightful blog posts, ChatGPT's versatility can help you project the best version of your professional self.

You just need to provide the AI with context. This includes your career objectives, skills, professional experiences, and other relevant information. Based on this, ChatGPT can draft a concise, professional description or even an entire blog post. Afterward, you can add your personal touch, making sure that the output accurately represents you before integrating it into your online profiles.

It's like having a personal assistant who understands your professional journey and helps you put it into words. Whether you're updating your LinkedIn bio or sharing industry thoughts on your blog, ChatGPT can support you in making a solid impression in the digital professional world.

Leveraging AI for Networking Event Preparation: The Power of ChatGPT

Networking events serve as a rich hub for connecting with industry professionals and potential employers, providing a platform to exchange ideas, explore opportunities, and foster meaningful relationships. To maximize the impact of these events, it's vital to come prepared with a succinct and impactful elevator pitch, foresee potential questions that could be directed toward you, and conceptualize engaging queries to pose to others.

ChatGPT, with its advanced language generation capabilities, is a powerful tool to assist in these preparations. Whether it's helping to craft a compelling elevator pitch that captures your professional journey and aspirations, simulating conversational scenarios to prepare you for real-life interactions, or brainstorming insightful questions to initiate engaging discussions, ChatGPT can play a vital role in your networking event preparation.

However, it's key to remember when utilizing ChatGPT the importance of personalization. While it is highly proficient in generating professional content and simulating conversations, it is crucial to adapt and modify the AI-generated output to reflect your voice, values, and unique circumstances genuinely.

This ensures that when you step into a networking event, you're not only well-prepared with your elevator pitch and potential questions but also confident in the authenticity of your communication. Thus, with ChatGPT by your side, you can approach networking events with greater confidence and purpose.

Adding a Personal Touch: Humanizing AI-drafted Emails

The most impactful emails are those that feel personal and human. While ChatGPT can help draft an email's structure and main points, adding your personal touch is crucial. This could include acknowledging a shared interest or connection, referring to a recent discussion or event, or expressing genuine enthusiasm or curiosity about something the recipient is involved in.

For example, if the recipient is someone you've met at a conference, you might mention a topic from their presentation that you found particularly insightful. Or, if you share an alma mater, you might refer to a common experience or tradition at your school.

Personalizing your communication not only makes it more engaging for the recipient but also helps to build a genuine relationship. In professional correspondence, as in all communication, showing that you see and value the other person as an individual can go a long way toward making a genuine connection and leaving a lasting impression.

Career Prompt Master: Setting the Tone for Effective Communication

Welcome back to the realm of prompts, where the power of effective communication lies at your fingertips! As the "Career Prompt Master," I'm here to guide you through the nuances of tone and its impact on your messages. While ChatGPT can generate impressive text, providing guidance on tone adds that extra touch of authenticity and ensures your communication hits the right note.

Tone plays a significant role in shaping how the recipient receives and interprets your message. To harness the true potential of ChatGPT, it's important to provide guidance on the desired tone for your emails. You can do this by suggesting specific words, phrases, or examples that reflect the tone you wish to convey.

From formal and professional to informal and friendly, the possibilities are vast. By crafting tone prompts, you become the conductor, orchestrating the perfect balance between words and emotions. Together, we'll explore various examples and guide ChatGPT to create emails that resonate with your unique communication style.

Here are a few examples of how you might provide guidance on tone to ChatGPT:

Formal Tone: "Dear ChatGPT, could you help me draft a formal email to a potential employer expressing my interest in the open role of data analyst at their company? I want to convey my qualifications, experience, and why I believe I'd be a great fit."

Informal Tone: "Hi, ChatGPT, I want to send an informal but professional follow-up email to a recruiter I met at a job fair. I want to thank them for their time, remind them of our conversation, and express my interest in the upcoming opportunities at their company."

Enthusiastic Tone: "Hey, ChatGPT, I need to write an email to my team sharing the good news of our project's approval. I want to express my excitement and gratitude for their hard work and motivate them for the upcoming tasks. Let's keep it enthusiastic and uplifting!"

Polite Tone: "ChatGPT, can you help me draft a polite email to a colleague asking for their feedback on the report I've prepared? I want to convey my appreciation for their insights and assure them that their constructive criticism is welcome."

Appreciative Tone: "Hello, ChatGPT, I want to write a thank you email to my mentor, who has been guiding me throughout my project. I want to convey my deep gratitude and appreciation for their invaluable support and guidance."

Striking the Right Note: Guiding ChatGPT toward Appropriate Email Tone

While ChatGPT's abilities in crafting human-like text are impressive, its performance can be further enhanced by providing guidance on the tone of your email. This could involve offering examples of the kind of tone you're aiming for or suggesting specific words or phrases for the AI to incorporate into its output. By doing so, you're helping shape the AI-generated content to better align with the context and purpose of your communication.

Remember, tone can significantly influence the way your message is received. Whether you want to come across as formal and respectful, casual and friendly, enthusiastic and passionate, or any other tone, your guidance can help steer ChatGPT toward creating an email that not only conveys your message but also does it in a way that aligns with your communication style and the situation at hand.

Language Unchained: ChatGPT Across Borders and Beyond Work

When it comes to language versatility and use-case diversity, ChatGPT doesn't disappoint. It's not just an English-language virtuoso; it has a way with several other languages too. As of its knowledge cutoff in September 2021, the AI model, can weave words in a multitude of languages, including Spanish, French, Italian, German, Dutch, Russian, and more. It's worth noting, though, that its prowess is strongest in English, given the high volume of English-language data used for its training.

But where ChatGPT truly breaks the chains is in its applicability beyond the professional sphere. Who said AI was all work and no play? Whether you need a hand with a personal email, you're in the mood for some creative storytelling, or you're simply brainstorming ideas for your next passion project, ChatGPT is here to help.

So, go ahead, and unleash the power of ChatGPT across languages and beyond professional confines.

AI Intervention: The Career Prompt Master's Networking Navigations

It's your friendly Career Prompt Master, here to guide you through the often-daunting labyrinth of networking and professional communication. In this chapter, we'll unlock the secrets of making meaningful connections using the power of ChatGPT.

Your first impression often sets the stage for your professional relationship, so it's essential to get it right. With my carefully crafted prompts and your unique voice, ChatGPT can help you draft personalized, engaging introductions and follow-up messages.

So, let's roll up our sleeves and get into the world of networking. Here are the Career Prompt Master's tips to help you make a lasting impression! Don't forget to tweak them to suit your unique style and needs. Happy networking!

Introducing Yourself: "Hello, my name is [Your Name], and I'm currently [current professional status]. I'm incredibly interested in [specific field or topic] and would love to learn more about your experience in this area. Could we schedule a time to discuss?"

Request for Informational Interview: "Hi, [Contact's Name], I came across your profile and was intrigued by your work in [their industry/field]. I'm keen on understanding more about [specific aspect of their work]. Would you be open to a brief informational interview?"

Asking for Advice: "Hello, [Contact's Name], I've always admired your work in [industry/field]. As I'm looking to navigate my own path in this sector, I'd appreciate any advice you could share about [specific topic or question]."

Building on a Common Connection: "Hi, [Contact's Name], we both worked with [mutual contact] at [company or event]. They mentioned your expertise in [specific area], and I would love to hear more about your insights and experiences."

Networking Event Follow-up: "Hello, [Contact's Name], it was a pleasure meeting you at [Networking Event]. I really enjoyed our conversation about [topic], and I was hoping we could continue our discussion over coffee sometime soon."

Connecting on Shared Interest: "Hello, [Contact's Name], I noticed we both have a keen interest in [shared interest or field]. I believe there's a lot we could learn from each other. Would you be open to a chat sometime soon?"

Offering Value: "Hi, [Contact's Name], I recently came across a [resource/article/book] that made me think of our shared interest in [topic]. I thought you might find it valuable and wanted to share it with you."

Collaboration Proposal: "Hello, [Contact's Name], I've been following your work and appreciate your expertise in [specific area]. I'm currently working on a project related to this, and I believe your insights could be quite beneficial. Would you be open to collaborating or discussing this further?"

Job Inquiry: "Hi, [Contact's Name], I noticed an open position at [their company] that aligns with my skill set and interests. I am considering applying and was wondering if you could tell me more about the company culture and your experience working there?"

Reconnecting with Old Contact: "Hello, [Contact's Name], it's been a while since we last connected at [previous interaction or shared experience]. I'd love to catch up and learn more about your recent work in [specific area]. Could we arrange a time to chat?"

The AI Advantage in Professional Networking

As we reach the end of Chapter 8, it's clear that ChatGPT isn't just an AI model—it's a game-changer in professional communication. It streamlines the creation of polished professional letters, enhances your online presence, prepares you for networking events, and extends its prowess beyond English and the professional sphere.

We've explored how, with the right prompts, ChatGPT can generate content tailored to various networking situations. The ten prompts shared are just the tip of the iceberg. The AI's potential to aid you in your professional journey is limited only by the quality of the prompts and the extent of your imagination.

As we've seen, technology, when used effectively, can open doors to new opportunities. Whether you're a seasoned professional or just starting your career, embracing these AI tools can significantly enhance your professional journey. And remember, in the world of networking and professional communication, every word counts. With AI like ChatGPT by your side, you're well-equipped to stand out from the crowd.

So, here's to embracing the AI advantage in professional networking. As we continue our journey in the next chapter, we'll take a closer look at how AI can be a potent tool skill development. Stay tuned!

CHAPTER 9
Continual Learning and Skill Development with ChatGPT

From AI to IQ: Elevating Skills with ChatGPT

In the accelerating pace of the professional world, staying at the cutting edge often means embracing continual learning. As a remarkable digital tool, ChatGPT can assist you in expanding your repertoire of skills and nurturing your professional growth.

Whether learning Python or practicing public speaking, ChatGPT is an incredible resource, always ready to serve. It can decode intricate concepts, generate practice problems, provide insights, and even engage in role-playing scenarios to facilitate your learning process.

Python Prowess: Coding with ChatGPT

For instance, if you're exploring Python, one of the most popular programming languages, you can have a coding conversation with ChatGPT. It can elucidate complex concepts, solve coding conundrums, or even generate Pythonic code snippets as examples. This real-time coding assistance can boost your understanding and proficiency in Python, catapulting your coding skills to new heights.

Eloquent Expression: Public Speaking Practice with ChatGPT

If you're looking to captivate audiences with your oratory skills, ChatGPT can come to your aid. You can use it to generate engaging speeches or simulate public speaking scenarios for practice. By offering instant feedback and suggestions, ChatGPT can help refine your public speaking skills, allowing you to deliver your messages confidently and effectively.

Reinventing the Wheel: Continual Professional Development with AI

In an era of unprecedented change, the mantra of success hinges on continual professional development. This process requires a commitment to ongoing learning—honing existing skills, acquiring new ones, and staying updated with industry advancements. ChatGPT can be a valuable ally in this journey, facilitating reflection, goal setting, and resource exploration.

Though ChatGPT doesn't possess real-time web access or database connectivity, it can offer a wealth of general advice and potential resources based on the patterns it has learned from a diverse array of internet text during training. This makes it a versatile tool for charting your professional development path.

The AI-Powered Tutor: Learning with ChatGPT

Envision ChatGPT as your personal AI tutor, ready to guide you through an array of subjects and complex concepts. You could delve into the intricacies of data science, explore the philosophies of ancient civilizations, or brush up on your managerial economics knowledge—ChatGPT stands by your side.

Whether you're keen on transitioning into a new field or enhancing your current professional capacity, ChatGPT can propose the skills typically valued in your chosen field, suggest potential learning paths, and even generate sample problems for practice.

AI-mpowering Your Professional Development Journey

Let's see how you can integrate AI into your professional growth journey and navigate the dynamic world of work.

ChatGPT can provide various types of general advice and potential resources for professional development. Here are some examples:

Skills Development: ChatGPT can generate a list of important skills for various roles or industries. For example, if you are interested in digital marketing, ChatGPT could suggest mastering SEO, Google AdWords, content creation, data analysis, etc.

Career Advancement: You can ask ChatGPT about common career paths in your chosen field or what steps you might need to take to progress. For instance, you might ask, "ChatGPT, what are the typical career progression steps for a software engineer?"

Learning Resources: While ChatGPT doesn't know specific documents or sources, it can provide general advice on the type of resources that might be helpful for learning new skills or topics. For instance, if you're trying to improve your leadership skills, it might suggest looking for books on leadership, attending workshops or seminars, finding a mentor, or seeking out online courses.

Interview Preparation: ChatGPT can generate responses to common interview questions, provide tips for successful interviews, and even help you role-play scenarios.

AI-ded Directions: The Career Prompt Master's Guide for Career Development

Hello there, the Career Prompt Master is back, this time with another set of beneficial prompts to assist you in your career development. Remember, these prompts are meant to provide guidance and spark conversations with ChatGPT, facilitating your path to career growth. Let's get started:

- "ChatGPT, can you list some key skills required for a successful career in [chosen field]?"
- "ChatGPT, could you provide a roadmap for transitioning from a career in [current field] to a career in [desired field]?"
- "ChatGPT, what are some resources for improving my skills in [desired skill]?"
- "ChatGPT, can you suggest a learning plan to acquire knowledge in [desired area]?"
- "ChatGPT, can you generate some interview questions that I might encounter for a role in [specific role]?"
- "ChatGPT, can you suggest some ways to showcase my proficiency in [specific skill] on my resume and cover letter?"
- "ChatGPT, could you provide tips for negotiating a higher salary or promotion?"
- "ChatGPT, how can I balance my professional and personal life better?"
- "ChatGPT, what steps should I take to prepare for a leadership role in my industry?"
- "ChatGPT, how can I maintain motivation and focus on my career goals?"

ChatGPT is a tool that can provide valuable insights and advice. Add it to a broader toolkit, including mentors, industry professionals, and personal research advice.

CHAPTER 10
Potential Limitations and Ethical Considerations of ChatGPT

Understanding the Limitations of AI in Your Job Search

While AI tools like ChatGPT offer numerous benefits, it's important to acknowledge their limitations. ChatGPT cannot access real-time information or updates, meaning it can't provide the latest job market trends or company-specific details.

Moreover, despite its sophisticated language generation capabilities, ChatGPT needs to truly understand the context and the nuances of human emotion and experience. As such, while it can generate insightful and helpful advice, it's not a replacement for human judgment, intuition, and personal experience in your job search.

Navigating the Ethical Labyrinth: AI in Job Applications

As AI continues to integrate into various aspects of our lives, including job applications and career development, it is crucial to consider the ethical implications of its use. These considerations range from maintaining authenticity and honest representation to privacy and data security issues.

Authenticity and Honesty: One of the paramount ethical concerns when using AI for job applications is maintaining authenticity. While AI can be instrumental in refining your resume, drafting cover letters, or preparing for interviews, ensuring that the end result accurately represents your abilities, skills, and experience is crucial. Using AI to generate qualifications or experiences that you don't possess might result in short-term gain but could have long-term negative consequences, including damage to your professional reputation.

Privacy and Data Security: The use of AI also introduces potential issues surrounding privacy and data security. It's crucial to understand how AI tools handle your data. While ChatGPT doesn't remember or store personal conversations, not all AI tools follow the same policy. Before using any AI tool, it's essential to review its privacy policies and understand how your data is handled. Always keep sensitive information secure and be cautious about sharing personal details, even when you're interacting with an AI.

Bias and Fairness: AI tools are trained on vast amounts of data, and they can unintentionally pick up and perpetuate biases present in their training data. This can lead to discriminatory outcomes in job applications. Companies should strive to use AI tools that are transparent about their training processes and actively work to mitigate potential biases.

In conclusion, while AI can be an immensely helpful tool in career development and job applications, it's essential to use it responsibly and ethically. Always ensure that your use of AI upholds honesty and authenticity, respects privacy and data security, and promotes fairness and inclusivity.

Embracing the Future: The Increasing Role of AI in the Job Market

As we step further into the digital age, the impact of AI on the job market is becoming more prominent. AI's potential to automate tasks, streamline processes, and generate insights is leading to significant shifts in job roles and the skills that are in demand.

How exactly will AI change the job market, and what specific tasks will it automate?

AI's primary effect on the job market lies in its ability to automate tasks, particularly those that are repetitive or data intensive. These can range from data analysis and report generation to customer service via chatbots and even more complex tasks such as diagnosing medical conditions. As a result, job roles are shifting, with less emphasis on routine tasks and more emphasis on tasks that require creativity, critical thinking, and complex problem-solving.

However, AI is not only about automation; it also allows for the creation of new roles and industries. As AI technology continues to develop, there will be an increasing need for AI specialists, data scientists, and ethical advisors to guide AI's implementation.

How can job seekers adapt to the increasing role of AI in their fields?

Job seekers can adapt to the increasing role of AI in several ways. One approach is to continually upgrade their skills and stay abreast of the latest developments in their field. This could involve learning how to work with AI tools or understanding the implications of AI for their industry.

Secondly, job seekers can focus on developing skills that are complementary to AI. These include critical thinking, creativity, leadership, and emotional intelligence, which are areas where humans continue to outperform AI.

Thirdly, job seekers can use AI to their advantage in their job search. AI tools like ChatGPT can help with tasks like drafting resumes, preparing for interviews, and researching potential employers.

In conclusion, while the rise of AI presents challenges, it also brings numerous opportunities. By staying adaptable, continually learning, and leveraging AI tools, job seekers can navigate the changing job market and excel in their careers.

CHAPTER 11
Embracing the Future of Job Seeking with AI

Summarizing the Benefits of Using AI in Job Seeking

Throughout this book, we've explored how AI, particularly ChatGPT, can be a powerful tool in job-seeking. From helping to draft professional resumes and cover letters to prepare for interviews, researching industries, planning careers, developing skills, and even navigating networking and communication, the potential benefits of AI are vast.

AI offers efficiency, accessibility, and personalization in job seeking. It can help you understand and articulate your career goals, sharpen your professional communication, and continually learn and adapt in a dynamic job market.

However, it's important to remember that AI is a tool to supplement human effort and judgment, not replace it. The most successful job seekers will be those who can effectively leverage AI while also bringing their unique human skills and insights to bear.

Tips on Staying Up to Date with AI Advancements

As AI continues to evolve, staying updated with the latest advancements is important. Following AI research organizations like OpenAI, attending AI conferences and webinars, participating in online AI communities, and subscribing to AI-focused newsletters can help you keep abreast of new developments.

Moreover, consider continual learning and skill development in AI. Even a basic understanding of how AI works can enhance your ability to use it effectively and stay ahead in the job market.

The Role of Humans in the Future Job Market

While AI has the potential to automate certain tasks, many aspects of work are distinctly human. Creativity, strategic thinking, leadership, emotional intelligence, and the ability to understand and navigate complex social dynamics are just a few examples.

As we move into the future, the job market will likely value these distinctly human skills even more. The key will be to find a balance—leveraging AI for efficiency and data-driven insights while honing and applying our human skills to solve complex problems, drive innovation, and lead teams.

The future of job seeking with AI is not just about adapting to a new tool, it's about embracing a new mindset. It's about recognizing AI's and human intelligence's unique strengths and understanding how they can complement each other for maximum benefit.

The Role of Humans in the Future Job Market

The rise of AI and automation has created some apprehension regarding job security as technology increasingly shows its capacity to carry out tasks traditionally performed by humans. However, while some tasks may be automated, there are many aspects of work that are inherently human. As we step into the future, understanding and leveraging these distinctly human skills will be crucial.

1. Harnessing Human Skills: AI excels at tasks that involve data processing and pattern recognition. However, human intelligence is characterized by traits like creativity, strategic thinking, leadership, emotional intelligence, and the ability to understand and navigate complex social dynamics. These capabilities allow us to conceive original ideas, understand nuanced problems, connect on a deep emotional level, and lead and inspire others. As we move into the future, the job market will likely value these skills even more, as they are the qualities that enable us to solve complex problems, drive innovation, and lead teams effectively.

2. Collaboration Between AI and Humans: AI and human intelligence are not competing entities but can complement each other to increase efficiency and productivity. While AI can handle repetitive tasks and analyze large volumes of data quickly, humans can apply critical thinking to interpret the data, make strategic decisions, and provide the emotional intelligence required in many situations. Therefore, the future job market will be about finding a balance—leveraging AI for efficiency and data-driven insights while honing and applying our human skills where they are most needed.

3. Embracing a New Mindset: The future of job seeking with AI is not merely about adapting to a new tool or technology. It's about embracing a new mindset, one that recognizes the unique strengths of both AI and human intelligence and understands how they can work together. This means learning how to use AI tools effectively but also focusing on the development of human skills that AI cannot replicate.

4. Lifelong Learning and Adaptability: With the rapid changes in technology, the job market will place a premium on adaptability and the willingness to engage in lifelong learning. As new technologies emerge and the nature of work evolves, continual learning and skill development will become increasingly important. This includes not just technical skills but also distinctly human skills that allow us to work effectively with others and bring a creative, human perspective to problem-solving.

While the role of AI in the job market will undoubtedly grow, the value of human skills will not diminish. Instead, the future will likely see a closer partnership between humans and AI, where each contributes their unique strengths to the shared goal of progress and productivity. By embracing this reality and preparing accordingly, we humans rest assured we will remain valuable contributors in the future job market.

NEXT STEPS
The Future is AI-mazing!

Embrace the Future and Harness the Power of AI

We've reached the end of our journey through the future of job seeking, but let's be honest, we're only just warming up. The rise of AI and automation might feel like stepping into unknown territory, but it's like unlocking a treasure chest of new opportunities.

Sure, change can be scary, but it's also thrilling. Every big tech shift in history has opened doors to new industries, jobs, and ways to work. The secret sauce? A can-do mindset and an appetite for lifelong learning. With these, you can do more than just ride the wave of change—you can surf it like a pro!

Believe in the human skills you bring—your creativity, emotional intelligence, leadership talents, and knack for strategic thinking. They're the magic ingredients that machines can't replicate, and they're going to stay golden in any future workplace.

As you kick off your job-seeking adventure, remember you're not flying solo. There are resources out there designed to help you navigate, offering nuggets of wisdom on everything from job search strategies to how to make AI your secret weapon in the job market.

If you enjoyed this book, why not swing by our website www.work-lifewin.com? We've got a ton of resources to back you up. We're here to equip you with the knowledge and skills to take on the future job market with gusto. Whether you need tips on resume writing, acing interviews, or you're curious about the power of AI in your job search, we've got your back.

Also, do check out the Work Life Win YouTube channel for an in-depth look into topics related to all aspects of career development offering engaging content to get you up to speed. Plus, you'll join a community of folks just like you, all geared up for career success in the AI age.

Oh, and we've got the Career Prompt Master! This handy assistant is ready to help, whether you're sprucing up your resume, prepping for an interview, or getting your head around the latest AI trends. The Career Prompt Master is right by your side, making your journey smoother and easier.

So, here's the bottom line: the future of job seeking isn't about choosing AI over humans or vice versa; it's about bringing out the best in both. So, embrace AI, sharpen those human skills, and stride confidently into the future.

Wishing you all the best on your career journey! We at Work Life Win, along with the Career Prompt Master, are cheering you on every step of the way. Let's harness the power of AI and carve out the career paths of the future.

Here's to your success! Let's do this!

Made in the USA
Coppell, TX
22 March 2024

30423802R00077